Passing

ALSO BY MICHAEL KORDA

MICHAEL KORDA

Passing

A Memoir of Love and Death

LIVERIGHT PUBLISHING CORPORATION

A Division of W. W. Norton & Company

Independent Publishers Since 1923

For information about permission to reproduce selections from
this book, write to Permissions, Liveright Publishing Corporation,
a division of W. W. Norton & Company, Inc.,
500 Fifth Avenue, New York, NY 10110

For information about special discounts for bulk purchases,
please contact W. W. Norton Special Sales at
specialsales@wwnorton.com or 800-233-4830

Manufacturing by LSC Communications, Harrisonburg
Book design by Ellen Cipriano
Production manager: Lauren Abbate

ISBN 978-1-63149-464-2

Liveright Publishing Corporation
500 Fifth Avenue, New York, N.Y. 10110
www.wwnorton.com

W. W. Norton & Company Ltd.
15 Carlisle Street, London W1D 3BS

1 2 3 4 5 6 7 8 9 0

For Margaret, always

We rarely go gentle into that good night.

—SHERWIN B. NULAND, *How We Die*

PART I

"I've known that something was
wrong for a long time."

1.

"YOU DON'T KNOW what you've got until it's gone," my wife Margaret was fond of saying, meaning that you shouldn't take the good things of your life for granted.

"When you see something you want, *go* for it," was also one of her maxims—she was never one for dithering or "shilly-shallying," as she put it. Hesitation was not part of her makeup, big life decisions or small ones alike she made quickly, without looking back, or regret afterward.

I was the more cautious one, inclined to think things out, or through. "Look before you leap," might have been my motto, a note of caution that was washed away by the fact that from the first moment I set eyes on Margaret I knew she was the woman I had always wanted. It was love at first sight—surely the most dangerous of emotions—and as I was shortly to discover it was mutual.

We met in 1972, of all improbably romantic ways while riding in New York's Central Park. I used to board a horse then at the one remaining stable near the park on West Eighty-Ninth Street and rode early every morning before taking the subway downtown to work. Margaret, a much more gifted and experienced rider, had started to rent a school horse in the mornings. Our rides were not synchronized, so for some days we went around the reservoir on the bridle path in different directions, merely saying good morning politely as we passed each other.

It was midwinter, so we had the bridle path pretty much to ourselves. The few riders who braved the weather went out in bulky down parkas suitable for a polar expedition; Margaret wore a sealskin coat with a silver fox collar, her long blond hair tucked up under a towering white fur cap, looking like Julie Christie in *Doctor Zhivago.* I soon learned she was married to Magnum photographer Burt Glinn, and not surprisingly that she was a model. I was married too. I could tell that this was going to be complicated, the mutual attraction was too strong for it to be otherwise, and soon we were riding around the reservoir side by side in the same direction, and stopping for a cup of coffee on the way to the B train.

By the spring we knew, or thought we knew, everything there was to know about each other, until one day when instead of stopping for a cup of coffee on Eighty-Sixth Street and Broadway, Margaret asked if I would like a cup of coffee in her apartment on Central Park West and I said yes, both of us knowing that the relationship was about to get even more complicated. Burt— by then my wife and I had become friends with the Glinns and we often went out to dinner together—was away photographing in Indonesia or somewhere, we had the apartment to ourselves. We forgot about the coffee, Margaret put Carly Simon's album *No Secrets* on, "You're So Vain" was the big hit of 1972, and we went into the bedroom and embraced passionately, just as I had been imagining for so long, at which point it became apparent that Margaret had left the Vuitton bag that accompanied her around the world in her locker at the stable, and with it her boot-jack. We fell on the bed, and Margaret said, "We've got to get our boots off."

In those days I still had a pair of riding boots made for me in

London by Henry Maxwell on Jermyn Street, tight enough that I needed to sprinkle talcum powder on the calves of my breeches before using boot pulls to haul them on, and Margaret's were, if anything, tighter. (English riding boots are *supposed* to fit like a second skin.) I told her to hold on hard to the headboard of the bed, got down on both knees, removed her spurs, and began to pull as hard as I could, to no effect. Without a bootjack there seemed no hope of getting them off. I stood up, she raised one leg, and I pulled harder. "I could cut them off," I suggested, but Margaret shook her head; she did not want to ruin a good pair of riding boots. From time to time Margaret lost her grip on the headboard and slipped to the floor, but after what seemed like hours I managed to get one of her boots off, then the second one popped off unexpectedly and I landed on the floor with a thump.

We both broke into laughter at the sight of ourselves in the mirror. I looked at my own boots. "To hell with the bedspread," Margaret said, and so we made love for the first time, Margaret in her riding breeches and me in my boots, and never looked back. For the next forty-five years we were each other's lover, companion, and best friend.

Margaret seemed invulnerable, her beauty and her athleticism untouched by age, her presence at once commanding, reserved, and slyly appealing, seemingly invulnerable. Even into her sixties she could still wear a bikini and look good in it, walk an hour a day in any weather, ride competitively and win—as a horsewoman she won the last of her five national championships at the age of sixty-six. She had never experienced a serious illness or any kind of surgery, not even the removal of her tonsils or her appendix, until 2011, when she had a melanoma removed from her right cheek, a scary moment, but one she managed to change into a kind of party, with friends coming from all over to sit and wait for her at New York–Presbyterian Hospital as the procedure was done under local anesthesia in the doctor's office while she was fully dressed, including her favorite pair of cowboy boots.

Unlike most people born in England, Margaret had perfect teeth despite a lifetime of drinking tea and eating too many "sweets," especially her favorites, Cadbury Fruit & Nut chocolate and Kit Kat bars. Age had weathered but not diminished Margaret's looks and sharpened the dramatic curve of the cheekbones; by 2016, she retained the agility of a young person and the perfect posture of the fashion model she once had been, she could still command attention when she entered a room. A lifetime spent outdoors—she could not bear being "cooped up" indoors during the daylight hours—had given her a kind of permanent tan. I was the one who had the big medical dramas over the years, two cancer surgeries and a cardiac arrest, while she remained virtually unscathed at the age of seventy-nine.

Nothing had therefore prepared us for the fact that we were standing outside a nondescript medical building in Poughkeepsie on April 1, 2016, of all dates, having just been told that Margaret had a large malignant brain tumor that might kill her in a matter of weeks if it wasn't taken care of at once.

The first step, the doctor told us, was to perform a biopsy of the tumor to find out what he was dealing with, and he could do the procedure the day after next—there was no time to waste. It was no big deal, he assured us, he would merely drill a small hole in the skull and take a tissue sample, then we would know exactly what we were facing.

I said that drilling a hole in the skull sounded like a pretty big deal to me, but that fell upon deaf ears. He was determined that we should realize the urgency of the matter, he told his secretary to give us an appointment card and a thick sheaf of forms to fill out, and dismissed us. We should read and sign everything before he saw us again on Friday.

Margaret's expression was that of a condemned prisoner looking at the firing squad with something between stoicism and hostility on her face as the neurosurgeon showed us the brain scan on his computer and pointed out the tumor, a glaring white blob on the left side of her brain, surrounded by an aureole of darker tissue. You couldn't really miss it. It looked like something glaringly out of place, which of course it was.

Once we were outside, she stared stonily at the Hudson River for a moment while we waited for the car, then she put her sunglasses on briskly, a signal that she was ready to move on. There were no tears on her cheeks, Margaret was not someone who cried easily. Until now I had always been the one who had needed nursing through one medical crisis or another, and it occurred to me that our roles had been suddenly reversed. "I knew it was going to be bad news," she said. Her accent was still English, hardly changed at all by more than five decades of living in the United States.

"Not this bad, surely?" I asked, but Margaret didn't answer. She was the one who faced bad news of whatever kind squarely, I was the one who tried to deliver it in small doses, trying to play it down, sugarcoat it. There was no way to sugarcoat this.

"Not this bad, no, but bad," she said as we stepped into the car. We held hands briefly. Hers was ice-cold, although it was a sunny spring afternoon.

I babbled on as we drove home. "He isn't the only neurosurgeon in the world, you know . . . The first thing we need is a second opinion. I'll call Adam. And Maurice. And Vinnie, of course . . ."

Adam Rosenblüth was Margaret's internist, Maurice Carter was her orthopedist, who over the years had always managed to get her back on a horse despite the inevitable aches and sprains of competition, both of them "in the city," as people said up here in Dutchess County as if New York City were Shangri-la, although it was only ninety miles away. Vincent Beltrani Jr. was our dermatologist, a friend and neighbor who collected and rebuilt old sports cars in his fully equipped garage, shared my passion for motorcycles, never failed to charm Margaret, and whom we had known since he was a teenager.

"I don't know a thing about brain tumors," I went on, "but I'll hunt up a few sites on the internet the moment we get home and read up on them, and try to find out which is the best hospital for this kind of thing . . ."

Margaret waited for me to run out of breath. She knew my way of processing bad news was to read up on whatever it was, then get on the telephone and start organizing things and people, the natural response of a retired book publisher. When faced with a crisis, my first instinct was to reach for my Rolodex and a telephone. "I've known that something was wrong for a long time," she said calmly.

~⌐◞

The truth was that I had half suspected so myself, although I had been reluctant to admit it and never imagined it could be anything this bad.

It had begun about a month ago, with Margaret dropping her whip while she was riding. She was a strong, gifted, fearless horsewoman, who rode two horses a day rain or shine, someone who had started riding in England at the age of three. In ordinary circumstances, even in extraordinary ones, she would never have dropped her whip, yet now day after day she did. When I could, I dismounted and handed it back to her, otherwise we came back later to look for it. I did not give it much thought, but I should have. It did not occur to me that she wasn't *dropping* the whip, it was slipping out of her fingers—she couldn't feel it.

She was a good driver too, her father's daughter in that respect, as in many others, but she had been driving faster than usual lately, and with a certain recklessness that sometimes made me nervous as a passenger, as if she weren't entirely sure where the right edge of the road was, or how close she was to other vehicles as she passed them.

A couple of weeks after she first began dropping her whip I began to notice that Margaret was slurring her words, so that I didn't always understand what she was saying. This was entering more difficult territory. I had been getting deafer as I aged, perhaps a legacy of two years in the Royal Air Force and two weeks in Budapest during the Hungarian Revolution of 1956, my hearing dulled by the noise of jet engines warming up in the age before hearing protectors were issued, and of artillery shells exploding close by, and I now depended on hearing aids, imperfect instruments at best. Margaret sometimes became impatient when I missed what she was saying, she urged me to get the hearing aids adjusted again, or get new ones, or "raise hell" with the audiologist. Then too, perhaps like most wives, she assumed that I simply wasn't *listening* to her, or perhaps still worse didn't want to hear what she had to say. In either case, the assumption was that it was my fault. My audiologist took all this calmly: "All wives complain about their husband's hearing aids," she said.

I felt guilty about this—and mildly resentful—but no matter how many times I went back to the long-suffering audiologist, the problem persisted and grew worse. It didn't occur to either of us that the problem might in part be *hers*—that she was groping for the right word and slurring it when she found it.

Other small changes came and went, some of them imperceptible to anyone but myself. Every afternoon around four we had tea, a familiar English institution, hers with sugar, mine without. One afternoon she tasted hers, put her mug down, made a face, and said, "This must be yours, there's sugar in it." I was about to tell her that she'd got it all wrong, in all the years I'd known her she had always put two spoonfuls of sugar in her tea, but something in her expression warned me not to. After all, what difference did it make? People's tastes change as they grow older, they suddenly "go off" things; still, it seemed strange that something as basic as this had changed. Margaret had always liked a lot of salt, but now she poured salt on her food with a lavish hand, so the saltcellar had to be filled up much more often than before. I did not imagine that changes might be going on in her brain that she did not even notice.

Margaret loved doing crossword puzzles, and excelled at it. Every afternoon after lunch she settled down with the *New York Times* crossword puzzle, a skill I do not have—she knew it was useless to ask for my help—and zipped through it with a ballpoint pen in time for tea. At some point, she switched to the much easier puzzles in the *Poughkeepsie Journal*, then gradually she stopped doing those too, the daily papers were left untouched.

She had been an avid reader of fiction too, marking off for me in the *New York Times Book Review* novels she wanted to read so I could get them for her, but now they piled up on the chest at the foot of the bed as if it were a secondhand bookshop. She could not concentrate, she thought she might need new reading glasses, but made no effort to have her eyes tested, and didn't respond well to my nagging her about it. She loved to read and reply to emails from her friends on her cell phone, but she found the phone harder and harder to work, and complained that the buttons on it were too small. She found it increasingly difficult to "do" her hair, or to fasten the clasp on jewelry, leaving me to come to her aid with clumsy fingers, to our mutual irritation.

Occasionally I told myself—after all, we had been together for over forty years—so this is what old age will be like, a succession of mild retreats from things that had once been easy. But then, at last, she turned to me as I made her a drink before dinner, and said quietly, "I think something serious is wrong with me."

My first instinct was to say, *Don't be silly,* but at the sight of her face I put that to one side. I finished making her vodka tonic, poured myself a glass of wine, and sat down opposite her at the kitchen table. "Wrong how?"

"I can't hold things, like a pen or an eyebrow pencil. I drop them. I don't even *know* I've dropped them. And I can't find the word I want. I'm embarrassed when I'm talking to people. Surely you've noticed?"

I nodded. I *had* noticed, and had chalked it up to fatigue or age—she would be seventy-nine in November, after all, four years younger than me. The closer you are to someone day by day, the harder it sometimes is to see that something is wrong. "I thought you were tired," I said, and it was true, Margaret *wasn't* sleeping well, and everything, even taking off her makeup before going to bed, seemed to take her more time and make her even more tired.

"It's not that. I'm sick. I need help."

⁓⸫

This was profoundly not in character. Except for what she called "maintenance," regular checkups and so on, Margaret tried to avoid doctors when possible, except for Maurice Carter, who had the gift of making a trip to his office seem like a social occasion. She had a typically English reluctance to seek out medical help, she was the opposite of a hypochondriac. Injuries that would have sent anyone else rushing to the nearest emergency room, Margaret ignored.

Once, when she was away trying out a horse in Massachusetts, the horse threw its head up and drove the metal frame of her Ray-Ban sunglasses deep into her nose. She washed the blood off, put several layers of cotton pads from the barn's horse first-aid kit over her nose, and drove more than two hours home alone in severe pain.

When I opened the front door and saw her that night I was appalled—once I had removed the bloodstained cotton pads I saw that the cut was deep, a ragged open gash, the flesh on either side bruised. It had not crossed her mind to call me, or to seek help. "I just need a Band-Aid," she said. With great difficulty I persuaded her to let me drive her to the emergency room of Vassar Brothers Medical Center in Poughkeepsie instead, where she was given an antibiotic and the wound was cleaned, then a plastic surgeon gave her a local anesthetic and did a terrific job of sewing it up with more than a dozen tiny stitches—we were lucky that he happened to be on call that night, because once it healed the scar was almost invisible. He too was amazed that she had driven two hours and proposed to put a dab of Neosporin and a Band-Aid on it when she got home. I thought, but did not say so, that if one of her horses had received a wound like that she would not have hesitated for a moment to call her vet, whatever time of the night it was.

That Margaret sought my advice instead of calling a doctor did not surprise me. When she competed she carried her own personal medical kit in the horse trailer, tranquilizers, painkillers, antibiotics, drugs to stop diarrhea or snuff out a cold, and when she needed advice about her health she was apt to seek it from those around her, like Roxanne Bacon, who looked after her horses, or her favorite equine veterinarian in those days, Paul Mountan, whose own dislike of seeking any kind of medical help was so great that rather than waste time visiting a dentist he once pulled out a painful tooth himself with a pair of pliers.

Margaret had grown up in a small English village in the days before the National Health Service, when the doctor still made house calls for routine matters and a visit to his surgery was something you only did for the most serious of health problems. Whatever childhood trauma had made her fear visiting a doctor, I never learned. Some of her best friends were doctors, but she sought unprofessional medical advice for as long as possible, and often asked me to serve as her go-between and describe her symptoms over the telephone. "Just tell him I need something for my cough," she would whisper to me, rather than asking herself. Not every doctor reacted well to this. Many of them told her to come into the city and see them, or even to take her own temperature, which she disliked doing in case it was higher than normal—she had a touching belief that a prescription containing codeine telephoned to her pharmacy would solve anything except a broken bone.

It was so unlike her to admit that she needed help that we sat for several moments in silence. "I don't want to go down to the city and make a big fuss of this," she said, holding her vodka tonic, but she sounded less sure of herself than usual. I recalled that she had recently had her yearly physical, but there had been nothing remarkable about her results. Her cholesterol level was a concern, which is common for someone her age, she took Pravachol for that, and her blood pressure was a little high—it always rose sharply when she was in a doctor's office, a reflection of her anxiety at the sight of any kind of medical apparatus, even a stethoscope. Otherwise Margaret's results were those of a person remarkably healthy for her age.

Could there be a problem with her medications, I wondered, her "pills," as she always referred to them? Ever since I had known her, almost forty years, Margaret had taken pills to help her sleep (currently Lorazepam and Clonazepam before bedtime), to calm her anxiety and control her depression (currently Effexor and Abilify at breakfast time). Over the decades the medications had been changed from time to time, as well as the dosage, but making sure that she had enough of her pills and that she had them with her if we were away from home was a first priority. She only took exactly what was prescribed, but they were an important part of her life, perhaps by now as much a matter of routine and habit as of need.

There was no mystery about Margaret's level of anxiety. On the contrary—she was a perfectionist, hard on herself, she worried about aging, losing her looks, what she would do with herself if she had to give up riding. Abilify was a fairly recent replacement for whatever she had been taking before, and might have been a mistake. People change, and so does their reaction to a new medication. "It could be a problem with your pills," I suggested.

Margaret shook her head. She looked on her pills as a lifeline, they were the last thing she would want to blame. She took a deep breath. "Do you think I could have had a small stroke?" she asked in a small voice.

The expression on her face was briefly one of terror. People who had strokes often become helpless, and if there was one thing Margaret feared, it was helplessness.

I said I didn't think so, surely she would have felt something, but the truth was that I didn't know. My maternal grandfather Octavius Musgrove had suffered a stroke at about the same age Margaret was now, but I remembered it as a full-scale medical emergency. He had been rushed to a hospital by ambulance, and when I visited him later on in the nursing home where he was sent to recuperate, which he never did, Ockie could not speak at all, his face was twisted to one side like that of a Picasso portrait, and he looked like a different person from the one I had known and loved.

"I need to know right away," Margaret said. "The sooner, the better."

"Let me call Dr. Tom, then, he'll know what to do." She nodded, clutching her untouched drink in her hand.

"Dr. Tom," as we always called Dr. Thomas Murray, a recently retired local ob-gyn doctor, had been a convivial friend of ours over many years, a man with whom we dined once or twice a month, if not more often.

Tall, ruddy-faced, and handsome, Tom Murray is not only a good doctor, but a boon companion who adored and admired Margaret, and therefore brought out the best in her. He has a sharp, boisterous sense of humor, very much like Margaret's, is a gifted storyteller and an instinctive flirt, and like her he loves horses, although his interest is horse racing rather than riding them. Like her, Dr. Tom loves British TV crime series and is a passionate reader of crime fiction—the two of them were constantly exchanging bags of books. Like me, he reads a lot of history, and is undaunted by long books with many footnotes. He is a connoisseur of good food, extra-dry vodka martinis, and beautiful women. In Tom's company Margaret could tease, laugh, gossip about the horse world, and enjoy herself to the point at which people sitting at the table next to ours sometimes asked to be moved to a quieter one. The mere mention of his name calmed her down at once. "Go ahead," she said, taking a sip of her drink. "Talk to Tom." Perhaps because he was *not* her doctor, Margaret had perfect faith in him.

I called Tom and he answered right away. After a little friendly chitchat I described Margaret's concern, trying to keep things as low-key as possible. Tom's voice dropped from its usual cheerful tone to the slightly more cautious one that any doctor uses when asked to give a diagnosis over the telephone about something that isn't his specialty for somebody who isn't his patient. He had seen

Margaret less than a week ago at dinner, she hadn't shown any
sign then of a stroke, a problem with her medications was certainly a possibility, what she needed was to see a neurologist,
he knew an excellent one and would ask him if he could fit us in
tomorrow. Margaret might think the neurologist looked a little
odd, he added, but he was first-rate.

By the time we reached the neurologist's office the next morning we were both in a state of nervous anxiety, alleviated in my
case by a certain curiosity to see what he looked like, and what
Dr. Tom meant by "odd." But the doctor, once he introduced
himself, did not seem particularly odd, except for his clothes—
sandals worn with socks, and clothes that looked as if they had
been collected from a Salvation Army bin. His manner was dif-
fident but professional. He asked Margaret to move her finger
from her nose to his finger, he tested her reflexes, he told her to
squeeze his fingers with her hands, none of which she appeared
to have any difficulty in doing; indeed, she squeezed his fingers
so hard that he winced. He did not think there was any reason to
suppose that she had had a stroke. He raised an eyebrow at the
list of medications she was taking—he too thought it was possible that the interaction of her medications might be causing the
problems she described, and would talk to her internist about it.
In the meantime, he said, it might be a sensible precaution for her
to have a brain scan just to rule out any other possibility. He did
not seem concerned, but since his office was close to where the
scan could be done we might just as well go over there and do it.
He would call and arrange everything, it wouldn't take long. His
manner—relaxed and reassuring—did not set off any alarm, even
for somebody whose alarm bells were so easily set off in a medical
setting as Margaret. He was as good as his word, and when we

got there we hardly had to wait at all. We attributed this to the neurologist's clout, rather than to any concern on his part about the possible severity of her case.

Margaret was instructed to change into a hospital gown and taken away to be given an IV—the procedure would take about three-quarters of an hour. I settled down to read the *New York Times*, and by the time I had finished it Margaret reappeared, looking none the worse for wear. It had not been difficult or in any way painful, she said, and she was glad to have it over with.

But it was not "over with." The wait for the results was interminable and inexplicable—we had yet to learn that the longer it takes to review a scan, the more likely it is bad news. No matter how many times I got up and went over to the desk to ask how much longer it would take, I could find out nothing. Margaret, usually the impatient one, was totally occupied in playing solitaire on her cell phone, despite her complaints about how small the buttons were. I recognized this as her own way of blocking out the reality of what was going on. Solitaire was her way of dealing with a delayed flight or a missed connection, or the many interminable waits at the U.S. Citizenship and Immigration Services office in New York City when we were applying for American citizenship.

The lady behind the desk was soon as fed up with me as I was with her. The radiologists were examining the scan, they were badly backed up, we would be called as soon as it was ready, I should sit down and wait until Margaret's name was called. I am normally an unnaturally patient person, but as the afternoon wore on I became testy, never a productive attitude in a medical setting. When would we have the disk of Margaret's MRI scan? The radiologists would get to it as soon as they could. Would they discuss it with us? No, they would give us a copy to take to the neurosurgeon, who would then talk to us. Why him? Because that's the way it is.

I placed a call on my cell phone to the office of the neurologist who had sent us here, and asked his secretary why we were being sent to another doctor instead of him. I had thought that we were supposed to bring the disk back to him? No, she said, the neurosurgeon was the one who would review it with us, it would also be scanned to her boss, I had misunderstood him, this was the normal routine, nothing to worry about. Finally, after what seemed like a lifetime, Margaret's name was called, and we were given a copy of the disk and sent to see the neurosurgeon.

Here, there were no crowds of patients, in fact the large, airy, empty white waiting room was eerily quiet. After what seemed like a long time, I went over to the sliding glass window behind which his secretary sat and asked when we might expect to see the doctor. He was just finishing a procedure, she said, he would be here as soon as it was done, and clacked her window shut firmly. I told Margaret. She sighed, and went back to her solitaire game. I thought she might get up and go home at any minute, but something kept her sitting there, and after a game or two more, at just the point when I began to fear she might get up and leave, the door opened and the secretary took us into the neurosurgeon's office.

He had a certain remote politeness, and seated us so that we were facing his computer screen, rather than himself. The only decoration on the walls was a huge late nineteenth century German colored print of a human brain, sliced about halfway through the skull, with every part neatly identified in German. His remoteness I understood. Margaret was not yet *his* patient, his job was merely to tell us about her scan. He was part of the medical equivalent of the military chain of command—the neurologist sends you to have a scan, the radiologist examines the scan, and sends it, together with his or her analysis, to the neurosurgeon, who then tells you what the scan shows. The system effectively prevents the radiologist from interacting with patients, which is perhaps exactly what it is intended to do, and why people become radiologists in the first place. We chatted briefly about Margaret's symptoms, her difficulty with finding the right words, and so on, and I handed him the disk I had been carrying like an offering. He waved it away; it had already been scanned to his computer. I saw now why we were sitting the way we were, the computer screen facing us, as if we were about to watch CNN together. He gestured toward it as if he were an impresario. "It's a large malignant brain tumor," he said, with the triumphant look of someone who has just dropped a bombshell into a conversation and brought it to a screeching halt.

Margaret stared at the screen silently, too shocked perhaps to say anything, then shut her eyes. I had no difficulty in guessing what she was thinking, that this was the end of the life she knew, that whatever was to come would consist of everything she hated, doctors, hospitals, surgery, physical disability, being indoors, that her life would henceforth be divided into two parts, before the diagnosis and after. As for me, it was déjà vu—when I was sixteen I had read John Gunther's *Death Be Not Proud*, a best-selling account of his sixteen-year-old son's doomed battle with brain cancer that was so vivid I read it twice. Gunther was a famous journalist, the author of *Inside U.S.A.* and a whole series of "*Inside*" books, and his descriptions of brain cancer—he was a brilliant reporter—etched themselves in my mind. I could still remember whole passages from the book, including the distinction between "encapsulated" tumors that can sometimes be removed easily "like a marble stuck in jelly," and "others . . . of an infiltrating spidery type that creep and burrow along the minute crevasses of the brain," as well the fact that any brain tumor the name of which begins with the prefix *glio* (from the Latin for "glue"), like *glioblastoma*, was "invariably fatal." Of course, much had no doubt changed in brain surgery in the sixty-five years since I had read the book, but I nevertheless managed to ask whether Margaret's tumor was encapsulated and how the doctor knew it was malignant. Could it be a glioblastoma? These were exactly the questions Gunther had asked.

The neurosurgeon gave a small sigh. *Death Be Not Proud* used to be on the curriculum of most high schools, so I may not have been the first layman in his experience to display more knowledge than I really had thanks to Gunther's book. The necrosis around the tumor, he said, pointing with his forefinger at a dark band around the white blob, makes it clear that the tumor is malignant and growing, the lighter gray band around that shows the brain swelling as the tumor mass expands . . . As for the kind of tumor it is, it was too early to say, that would have to be determined by a biopsy. He warmed ever so slightly to his subject. As we could see, the tumor was on the left side of the brain, since the left side of the brain controls the right side of the body, which explained the problems with Margaret's right hand, as well as her difficulty in finding words, because the left side of the brain also controls language and speech . . .

A pause. Did we have any questions?

I could see that Margaret was simply numbed by the news, and frozen by the lecture. I leaned over and put my arm around her—I would have to ask the questions for her. Would Margaret need brain surgery? was the first and most obvious one. The surgeon made a steeple of his fingers and stared over my head at the wall as if he were searching for the answer there. He pursed his lips. He could not say for sure until after seeing the results of the biopsy, but we should bear in mind that removing a tumor of this size might have a significant effect on her "quality of life."

This was a song I had heard before, when I was about to undergo a radical prostatectomy at Johns Hopkins. When a surgeon of any kind talks about quality of life it is time to start worrying about the future. It also occurred to me that Margaret's definition of quality of life might be very different from that of the neurosurgeon's—anything that prevented her from riding her horses with the wind in her hair would not seem to her a life with any quality at all.

Did that mean it was inoperable? I asked. He shook his head, no, not necessarily, but the biopsy was the first step, the sooner, the better.

We should have no concern about the biopsy, the neurosurgeon went on, it was a simple procedure that would tell him everything he needed to know. He described the process briefly. There were a couple of spots of concern on the lungs, he added, as he rose to show us out, but we should not think about them now, the main thing was to get the brain tumor biopsied at once, then we could decide how to go forward. I do not think Margaret heard him, she was still in shock, certainly she had no reaction, and in fact he passed over the subject of "spots of concern" so quickly that it hardly registered with me until much later.

Would she have to have her head shaved? Margaret asked.

Just a tiny spot, he replied with some impatience. Her hair should not be her first concern, there were bigger and more serious ones than that. I could see he thought, quite wrongly, that Margaret either didn't understand the gravity of what he had told her or didn't take him seriously, but I recognized it as an altogether sensible question from her point of view. She had absorbed the bad news with her usual stoicism—her health, her life were at risk, she understood all that, but still she wanted to be reassured about what it would do to her appearance.

It was not a question of vanity; her long blond hair was part of who she was, something she would think about even in the midst of a disaster. The first thing Margaret asked at any place we went to was where she could plug in her hair dryer—over the years I had filled a black leather zip bag with an assortment of adapters for every imaginable electric outlet and voltage in the world, two-prong, three-prong, you name it, it was an essential part of her travel kit, Margaret's hair dryer had blown fuses and caused blackouts in hotels, motels, and safari camps on every continent. To me, her question was a healthy sign that she had not been totally knocked out by the news, but the doctor may have taken it as a sign that she was on the verge of hysteria and about to become difficult. He herded us swiftly and efficiently out of his office and passed us on to his secretary, who was waiting with a thick sheaf of paperwork for us to take home with us.

From the rigidity of Margaret's face and her body, her back straight as a drill sergeant's, shoulders squared, mouth set, I could tell that she was holding back tears. Whether of anger, fear, or just plain shock at bad news presented so abruptly was hard to tell.

"Let's go home," she said.

2.

ONCE WE WERE home, Margaret went to the barn to see her horses. She derived a kind of comfort from their presence. They could not be cuddled with like cats and don't project total devotion and loyalty as many dogs do, but Margaret would place her head against the shoulder of one of them and somehow draw from the horse a degree of sympathy that most people would not. Her horses calmed her even at her most anxious moments in a way that nothing else could. I knew better than to intrude, so I went to my office and began to draw up a list of the people I needed to call.

It quickly grew to a daunting length. I put it to one side for the moment and began to go through the thick wad of papers I had brought home, separating the ones that Margaret would need to sign and the forms that would have to be filled out. To my surprise, there was a copy of the radiologist's report. I began to read it, with the kind of guilty feeling that accompanies reading someone else's mail. Some of it was above my head, other parts I could tease the meaning out of in layman's terms. "There is a mass in the left mid parietal lobe . . . This mass has both solid and necrotic components and vasogenic edema as well as evidence of prior hemorrhage . . . This may represent a primary brain neoplasm such as, but not limited to, an astrocytoma or glioblastoma multiforme but a metastasis cannot be excluded based on this exam."

The words "vasogenic edema" stumped me momentarily, but after looking up the phrase, I took it to mean swelling. The tumor had been there for some time, I surmised, and growing, and was surrounded by dead cells and fluid, together with blood from a "prior hemorrhage," all that was clear enough, however dismaying. I wondered if the "prior hemorrhage" had been responsible for Margaret's difficulties with using the fingers of her right hand. Remembering John Gunther, I knew an astrocytoma was bad news, a glioblastoma was fatal news, and there was a difference between "primary" brain tumors—that is, those formed in the brain but which do not travel elsewhere—and metastatic brain tumors, which have been formed by cancer cells traveling from elsewhere in the body and are very bad news indeed. "Mass effect" I understood vaguely. As the tumor grew it pushed away the healthy brain tissue to make room for itself, but what really caught my eye was the *size* of the tumor: "3.5 x 2.7 x 3.4 cm in size."

At first I thought I had misread it and mistaken millimeters for centimeters, but I read it again, and there was no doubt which it was. I had attended school in Switzerland, but those of us there who were British or American still clung to our own archaic system of measurement since it would be needed for our college or university entrance test, so even at this late stage of my life my mind did not easily visualize objects, distance, temperature, weight, or volume measured in metric units. My mind still functioned in pints and inches, not liters and centimeters.

I pulled out a ruler, measured off three and a half centimeters, and my stomach lurched as I came to grips with the fact that the tumor in Margaret's brain was not much less in volume than a ping-pong ball. This was a large mass to imagine growing in the tightly packed interior of Margaret's skull.

I skimmed through the rest of the report, most of it describing the results as "unremarkable," only to notice under "Lungs/ Pleura" a brief note of "a 7mm nodule in the left lower lobe," a "6mm nodule in the right lower lobe," a "questionable 7mm nodule in posterior of the right lung base," and "a 7 x 9mm cystic lesion" in the pancreas. These were presumably "the couple of spots of concern" the doctor had mentioned as we were leaving. I paused to consider the possibility that Margaret's problem might be more widespread than her brain tumor, frightening though that thought was.

The first question, of course, was whether or not to share all this with Margaret, but it seemed obvious to me that she already had enough to deal with at the moment. She had to absorb the news that she had a malignant brain tumor, as well as the idea of having a brain biopsy that entailed drilling a hole through her skull the day after tomorrow. It was difficult to know whether she had heard the neurosurgeon's remark about the presence of other tumors in her body, or if that had simply not registered in the shock of learning about the malignant brain tumor. Either way, there did not seem anything to be gained by reading her the radiologist's report or explaining what it meant in detail, even had I been equipped to do so.

I slipped the radiologist's report to the bottom of the pile of papers on my desk (and with some degree of guilt shelved it at the back of my mind for the moment) and began to fill out the forms—previous medical history, current medications, insurance information—all of which was soon going to become second nature to me over the next year, so much so that I took to carrying the information around with me in a special briefcase, together with my reading glasses and a ballpoint pen, to speed up the process of filling out forms on a clipboard in innumerable doctor's and hospital waiting rooms.

I thought what we needed was a second opinion, but we needed it fast—the neurosurgeon's reaction to Margaret's brain scan made it clear that delay was not an option. When I had been diagnosed with prostate cancer in 1994, Margaret and I sought out second opinions from surgeons in New York City, Boston, and Baltimore, but there was time to spare, nobody suggested that a week or two one way or the other would make any difference, prostate cancer is usually slow-growing. When I finally chose Johns Hopkins in Baltimore it was on the recommendation of numerous friends, one of whom declared passionately that he would "lie down in the street in front of traffic" to stop me from going anywhere else. Despite this offer of self-sacrifice I had always believed since that I made the wrong choice, that Memorial Sloan Kettering Cancer Center in New York City would have been better by far (admittedly this comes under the category of not crying over spilled milk), but I could not complain that we didn't get an opinion from enough eminent urologists before reaching a decision. Getting a second opinion from distinguished specialists of any kind is usually a long, slow process; it's hard enough to even get an appointment with one, let alone travel to Boston to see whoever is reputed to be the best neurosurgeon at Massachusetts General Hospital, or to Rochester, Minnesota, to see his or her counterpart at the Mayo Clinic. Nor are specialists necessarily sympathetic to "doctor-shopping," even if we had the time to do it. Besides, while almost every man over the age of fifty has a recommendation to make about a urologist, not many people have a favorite neurosurgeon.

As I looked through the scribbled notes of people I needed to call, a name on one slip of paper caught my attention: Dr. Alain C. J. de Lotbinière. Margaret's diagnosis had altogether erased from my mind the fact that I was scheduled to speak about *Hero*, my biography of Lawrence of Arabia, at a book club dinner being held at the Kittle House, a restaurant in Chappaqua, New York, on Monday evening next week, an event that had been arranged months ago. The invitation had come from Dr. de Lotbinière. Whatever was going to happen, it was clear to me that I was probably not going to be giving a talk about T. E. Lawrence Monday night.

No author likes to cancel an event at the last moment that was arranged months in advance. It happens, of course, in our part of the country everybody understands that events scheduled during the winter are dependent on the weather—a snowstorm that shuts down the Taconic Parkway cancels all obligations—but perhaps because my mother was an actress the tradition that "the show must go on" had a certain resonance for me. Come to that, Margaret was not someone who would normally let bad weather or illness cancel her plans. I was fairly sure that if I asked her she would tell me to carry on, but who could foresee what we might be doing four days from now?

I picked up the telephone to call the organizer of the event, remembering as I did so that Dr. de Lotbinière—and his father—had attended the same boarding school that I did in Switzerland, indeed that had been the reason I accepted his invitation to speak about Lawrence to his group in the first place, even though my biography of him had been published six years ago. Among those who attended Le Rosey "the old school tie" remained figuratively and literally a strong bond, not something to be taken lightly. Apart from "sportsmanship," one of the basic principles that had been drummed into us in several languages at Le Rosey was that when a Roséen said he was going to do something, he must do it.

I had several numbers for Alain de Lotbinière, but I remembered that he had told me to use that of his cell phone if I needed to reach him. He answered at the first ring, in a sonorous, low-pitched, polite, and even soothing voice, with no more than the slightest suggestion that he was, at the very least, trilingual, but then so are most people who have gone to a boarding school in Switzerland. After he had told me how much he was looking forward to Monday night I told him, with some embarrassment, that I was calling to say that I could not be there. Why? he asked, without any trace of the impatience he must surely have felt at my canceling my appearance at an event that had been planned so far in advance. I explained that Margaret had been diagnosed with a malignant brain tumor, and that I would surely have other things on my mind this coming Monday than Lawrence's hopes for the Middle East in 1919.

Yes, he replied in the same calm, soothing voice, of course he could understand that. The other members would be disappointed, but many of them were doctors, they would understand. We could put Lawrence off to a later date, when Mrs. Korda's problem had been resolved. I explained that as yet we had no idea of what was in store for her, or how we would deal with it.

That was only to be expected, he said, and perhaps he could be of some help—he was himself, as it happened, a neurosurgeon of some experience. It came back to me quite suddenly that of course I knew that. It had not seemed to me important at the time, but I recalled that Alain de Lotbinière's emails came from Brain & Spine Surgeons of New York, in White Plains. He was not just a neurosurgeon, but a distinguished one, medical director of the Cancer Treatment and Wellness Center at Northern Westchester Hospital, an associate professor of neurosurgery at Yale University Hospital for seventeen years, with a string of initials after his name. I had looked him up when he first called, then promptly put it out of my mind since I had not imagined that either of us would be in need of a brain surgeon.

De Lotbinière understood the need for urgency without my mentioning it. He would make time to see us at eleven fifteen a.m. the day after tomorrow, he said. I should bring Margaret's brain scan with me. He would not mind at all giving us a frank second opinion, or our seeking another one afterward, although he too urged me not to waste time—a malignant brain tumor was a very serious matter.

"By the way," he added, "whatever you decide to do, until I have reviewed the scan myself, *don't let her have a brain biopsy.*"

I tend to make friends instantly; Margaret's instinct was more cautious. Once she had made a friend, he or she remained one for life, but she had a certain skepticism when it came to my sudden enthusiasms for somebody new. Although Margaret sometimes looked imperious to strangers, she was in fact rather shy, very English in the way she did not open up immediately to people she had just met—it took a while before her robust sense of humor and friendliness shone through. Ordinarily, she might not have been swept away by my conviction that Dr. de Lotbinière was the right man for her to see, and sensibly she put very little faith in the fact that he had been to the same boarding school as me—the bond of "the old school tie" carried no weight for her—but she had not liked the neurosurgeon we had seen in Poughkeepsie, and in any case preferred making a trip down to Mount Kisco and back for a consultation to having a hole drilled in her head. After all, who wouldn't?

I dealt with the delicate task of letting the neurosurgeon in Poughkeepsie know that we were going to seek a second opinion and that Margaret would therefore not be coming for a biopsy on Thursday morning—fortunately I was able to leave a message, rather than having to argue about the merits of a brain biopsy with him.

The next day might have been idyllic, had it not been for Margaret's diagnosis. I was, atypically, at loose ends, having called Mary Higgins Clark, whose editor I had been for over fifty books, early that morning to explain that I could not attend the lunch celebrating the publication of her latest novel, *As Time Goes By*, the first time I had missed one in forty years. Margaret thought I should have gone anyway, but it would have meant my being away for the whole day, and I was uncomfortable with the idea. The thought had crossed my mind—and surely hers—that there was no knowing how many more days like this we would have together. It was beautiful spring weather. We rode together, walked a couple of miles, and in the afternoon Margaret drove to Rhinebeck for a manicure, as she did every Wednesday, followed by an early dinner in the Tavern of the Beekman Arms, which we always enjoyed.

It would not have been in keeping with Margaret's character to display any sign of nerves. The British war poster of 1939 and 1940 might have been written with her in mind, "Keep Calm and Carry On," words that summed up a whole outlook on life. Whatever might be going on in Margaret's mind, she would not want to display fear, although I could not help noticing that the fingers of her right hand were trembling ever so slightly, so that her knife rattled against the edge of her plate.

It wasn't something she could control, I do not even think she was aware of it. It was not her mind that was making her fingers tremble, I know now that it was simply the tumor pressing on the left side of her brain, sending messages from the left mid parietal lobe down through the spiderweb of nerves to the fingers of her right hand. She couldn't have stopped them if she tried. It was as if the cancer had a life of its own, which of course it did. It had moved from her right cheek to her lungs, and perhaps to her pancreas in the form of microscopic dots seeking a home, nesting there for years without doing any harm until they gained enough strength or vitality or life force to migrate through the bloodstream, past the blood-brain barrier that is supposed to protect the brain from almost every threat *but* metastatic cancer, to nestle in a place where the cancer could grow unimpeded without causing pain (the brain feels none) or, for some time, symptoms. Metastatic melanoma is, as oncologists often describe it, "a ticking time bomb" in the body. It bides its time, then years after you may have been told that the dermatological surgeon "got it all," it explodes where you least expected it, far from the original site on the skin, inside the brain, for example. It can wait ten or eleven years or more, during which time you think you're safe, having no symptoms, but given time a few stray cells are enough to kill you.

We tried not to talk about Margaret's illness at dinner, although it took a conscious effort. As we were to discover, the tumor would soon become the proverbial "elephant in the room," too big to ignore, more difficult still to pretend it isn't there. Cancer not only takes over the body, it takes over your whole life if you let it. Margaret understood that, she had learned from my own brush with cancer the importance of trying to cling to one's normal interests and routine for as long as possible. It was not a question of ignoring the disease or pretending it wasn't happening, she was far too realistic for that, but she understood that the disease was the enemy, you had to prevent it from taking over your life to the exclusion of everything else for as long as you could.

When I had been recovering from cancer surgery at home twenty-two years ago and was still wearing a dressing gown to conceal the catheter and the bag attached to my leg, she made sure to invite for dinner friends from the city who would talk about politics, book publishing gossip, history, anything except what she called "cancer talk," and now that she herself was faced with a far more serious and threatening problem than mine had been she was determined not to let the cancer become our only subject of conversation.

This was wisdom rather than escapism; we had learned it the hard way. With considerable effort we ate our crab cakes and talked about horses, movies, television, anything but what we both had on our mind.

⁓

The Cancer Treatment and Wellness Center at Northern Westchester Hospital in Mount Kisco, New York, is a separate two-story red-brick building with an entrance more like that of a hotel than a hospital. I had vaguely assumed that "Mount Kisco" was a geographical feature from the Old Testament like Mount Sinai, but in fact it was merely a poor transliteration of an Indian word for mud, a mistake made in about 1700. Mount Kisco today is a prosperous commercial center in Westchester surrounded by horse farms and big estates, something of a bridge linking expensive country homes to more modest suburban ones.

The two women at the admissions desk of the Cancer Treatment and Wellness Center showed exemplary patience as I filled out the forms—they smiled and made eye contact, and remembered our names, a very different experience from those who dealt with patients elsewhere from behind a glass window that they slammed shut as soon as they could. Here, the tone seemed friendly and informal, very unlike a hospital. I noticed that they each had their own pronunciation of Dr. de Lotbinière's name, not surprisingly, and tended to refer to him for simplicity's sake as "Dr. D."

Once we were ushered inside, the center had a strangely soothing and cheerful look to it. There were big overstuffed armchairs and sofas, each with its own brightly patterned pillow, set around a large table with the latest magazines spread neatly on it, not the untidy piles of ancient, dog-eared copies of *Reader's Digest* like those in most hospital waiting rooms. The colors were warm pastels, chosen no doubt to have a calming effect on patients and their family. There was a large aquarium full of brightly colored tropical fish and a long table with an urn of citrus-flavored water, hot water for tea and coffee, even a plate of cookies. In the background there was soothing music, rows of well-tended plants and flowers, the lighting was subdued, everything had clearly been selected with considerable care to reduce anxiety and create a sense of well-being. Here, there were no long rows of nervous or distressed patients sitting on uncomfortable hard plastic chairs against bright white walls waiting for their name to be called out—in fact there were only a few people here, seated comfortably in the big armchairs and looking about as relaxed as anyone can be in a cancer treatment center.

None of this tasteful décor seemed likely to altogether calm Margaret's anxiety, but the surroundings held it to a sustainable level, there was nothing visible to alarm her, the background seemed hardly medical at all. The music was low and classical, and I was not surprised to read on the bulletin board that a harpist played here at certain times of the day. I recognized that all this had been carefully thought out, and as well that all the cookies and plants in the world could not alter the reality of what was concealed behind the polished wooden doors, but I could not help reflecting that there was a real and important statement being made here—there is no reason to treat those who have cancer as if they are army recruits in institutionalized settings that are only one step above a prison. Recognizing their need to be treated with care, dignity, and respect is the first step in dealing with their illness, even small touches can make the experience less distressing.

In keeping with the atmosphere of the place Dr. de Lotbinière himself appeared to greet us, rather than our being ushered into his office by his nurse or one of the receptionists. He was tall, well dressed, courteous, cheerful, even jovial, there was nothing forbidding about him at all. I could not help noticing that he wore a well-cut suit rather than a white doctor's coat, and narrow, elegant, beautiful polished shoes, looking every inch like what an old Rosean should be. He charmed Margaret at once, treating her as if she were a guest to a party. I thought he might be about to kiss her hand—at school we had been expected to kiss the hand of the headmaster's wife every evening as we filed out after dinner—but instead he gestured her toward the most comfortable chair. I gave him the disk of Margaret's brain scan, and he turned to his right to study it. His computer was off to one side, so the three of us sat comfortably looking at each other, as if we were about to have tea. When he wanted us to look at something I stood up and looked over his left shoulder, while Margaret, who was closer, remained seated as he isolated a feature and enlarged it for us. His manner was calm and reassuring, unlike the previous neurosurgeon we had seen he was informative and low-key, and he succeeded at once in thawing Margaret. She had not even wanted to look at the scan the last time it had been shown to her, in fact she had kept her eyes firmly shut, but this time she looked at it attentively, and even asked a few questions. He answered them quietly, without drama, his description of the tumor not so very different from that of the radiologist's report, although shaded a little more gently.

Of course, Margaret had not read that report, which was buried on my desk, so she was hearing about it in detail for the first time. Coming from Dr. D it did not appear to frighten her, she listened calmly, without any evidence of anxiety, her chin resting on her hand—he could hardly have had a more perfect "bedside manner," the old-fashioned way of describing a doctor who knows how to talk to a patient, had he been a general practitioner on a house call telling her to take a couple of aspirin, spend a day or two in bed and take plenty of liquids, rather than a brain surgeon with the full range of modern science and surgery at his fingertips. No doubt he realized at once how much Margaret feared and hated the idea of becoming a patient, acted upon rather than acting, giving up control, handing over to him or anyone else with a stethoscope the life she had built for herself so carefully over the years. She had a natural reluctance to put that life in the hands of any doctor, even one so gentle and charming in manner, a reluctance intensified by a lifelong fear of the medical profession, but she was struggling to overcome it. She would henceforth call him "Dr. Alain" to avoid the difficulty of pronouncing his last name.

Why was he against her having a biopsy? she asked. He gave a gentle shrug. At this point it doesn't matter what *kind* of tumor it is, he told her, what matters is to remove it at once. When that has been done, it will be biopsied, of course, but the important thing now was to remove it. There was no point in making two holes in the skull, one for a biopsy, another later on for surgery. In addition, there was always some danger that the biopsy might cause a hemorrhage as it pierced the tumor, so why run the risk? That made evident good sense to me, and apparently to Margaret too. There is, in fact, an old neurosurgeon's adage, "It's much more important to know *where* something is than *what* it is." I had found this searching on the internet about neurosurgery, and clearly it still held true.

It was apparent from her questions that Margaret had reconciled herself to the surgery. She had decided to trust Dr. Alain, and as I well knew, once she made a decision she never looked back on it. How long would the surgery take? she wanted to know. At least four hours, maybe more. We must understand that this was *major* surgery—he firmly emphasized the word. Gently, he touched the left side of her head with his fingertips a couple of inches above the ear and indicated a sweeping crescent with his index finger. He would make an incision here, lift out a piece of the skull, then remove as much of the tumor as he could. Margaret did not flinch, she merely asked how much of her hair she would lose. Dr. Alain took this in his stride, he was a man of the world, he did not dismiss Margaret's concern for her hair. He would merely have to remove a narrow strip of hair, he reassured her, indicating about an inch with his thumb and forefinger. She nodded. He had passed the first test.

The next would be harder, I guessed. Would she ever be able to do the things she loved, riding, taking long walks, dinner with friends? she asked. This was the nitty-gritty for Margaret, I knew that.

Unlike the previous neurosurgeon, Dr. Alain kept eye contact with his patient, he looked at Margaret steadily and with sympathy. The aim was to restore and preserve her quality of life, he replied. Coming from Dr. Alain, the words "quality of life" sounded more like a promise, however qualified, than a threat. There were risks associated with this kind of surgery, it would be foolish to deny it, he went on, there could be no guarantee, but he saw no reason why she should not eventually resume doing the things she loved.

He did not overburden Margaret with the physical details of the surgery he would perform; she did not want to know them, nor probably do most other patients facing brain surgery. She already guessed without being told that despite the precision and delicacy involved in performing a craniotomy and the resection of a brain tumor, it was still a bloody and challenging procedure. If you let your mind wander there, you only have to imagine the surgeon cutting through your scalp, drilling holes into your skull, sawing between them, removing a piece of it, then cutting into that portion of your brain where speech, right hand movement, and so much more of what is "yourself" are contained—what neurosurgeons call the "eloquent" portion of the brain. Margaret was consenting, whether she knew it or not, to let Dr. Alain perform surgery in the part of her brain that defined and controlled the very essence of who she was.

Of course, whenever a surgeon needs to operate you cannot help imagining what life will be like if things go wrong, leaving to one side the question of whether you survive, but with brain surgery you also have to wonder whether you will emerge from it as the person you were—not just whether you will be able to ride a horse, drive a car, cook dinner, or play Scrabble, but whether your memories, your feelings, your sense of self will be intact. What if some or all of that intricate web of knowledge, experience, character, personal tastes, and personality is lost in the process, who, what will you be? To Dr. Alain's credit, he did not play down the risks, but he somehow managed to make it clear that he was on her side—not a threatening medical authority figure, but a friend. In these circumstances this was no mean achievement.

At home, while Margaret was asleep, I had watched some parts of a color videotape of a craniotomy performed by Dr. Brett Osborn, which was boldly, and as I soon learned accurately, marked with the warning, "This is not for the faint-hearted." That was putting it mildly. Once the skull is opened, brain surgery is a delicate art—it must take nerves of steel and the fingers of a concert pianist to cut into the brain itself—but opening the skull resembles carpentry carried out with a high-speed drill in a torrent of blood, saline solution, and fine bone dust. Watching Dr. Osborn, a passionate weight lifter and motorcyclist, drill half-inch holes in the skull, saw between them to detach a piece of it, then lift it out to reveal the brain below was an amazing but gruesome experience for a layman, at any rate it was for me. Imagining this being done to someone you love (and keeping it to yourself) is harder still.

Having gained Margaret's confidence, Dr. Alain skillfully gave us a brisk foretaste of the future. He would perform the surgery at Westchester Medical Center University Hospital (henceforth referred to as WMC), in Valhalla, New York, which was just over an hour away from our farm by car. After surgery Margaret would have to spend a few days—it was impossible to predict how many—in the Neurological Intensive Care Unit. Margaret wanted to know how long it would be before she could go home. Dr. Alain patiently deflected this question. It was impossible to say for sure. She might benefit from a period of rehabilitation, a transition toward her return home. I could see from Margaret's expression that this was going to be a sticking point, and so could Dr. Alain, who waved it away—we would have to see how much progress Margaret made in the Neuro-ICU. Once she was home, she would need some level of outpatient rehabilitation therapy, either at home or at a local hospital, and once she had sufficiently recovered he would administer "Gamma Knife radiation," a very precisely targeted radiation intended to kill any remaining cancer cells in the "bed" of the tumor, that is to say the place in the brain from which the tumor had been removed.

The word *knife* caused Margaret to frown momentarily, but in fact no knife was involved, he explained, it was a painless and simple process, she should have no anxiety about it. He moved from Margaret's brain scan on his computer screen to his calendar. He would be able to perform the surgery in two weeks' time, on Wednesday, April 20. I had hoped it would be sooner, but Wednesday was the day on which he operated, and his schedule was already full for next week. I expected Margaret to object or to ask a few more questions, but instead she just looked intently at Dr. Alain and said, "Wednesday is good for me."

And that was that. I knew Margaret well enough to tell that she had made up her mind, and nothing would change it— nothing ever changed her mind once she had made it up. Whatever her misgivings, she had accepted that she was going to have the surgery, and she had decided on Dr. Alain, there would be no doctor shopping, no hesitation, no second thoughts. Once Margaret had decided to take a fence she rode full-tilt at it, without fear, without doubt. Her motto had always been that of the great American horseman Harry deLeyer (rider of the famous show jumper Snowman): "Throw your heart over the fence and the horse will follow."

Neither of us had any idea how high that fence would be.

3.

If you don't know where you are going,
any road will take you there.

—LEWIS CARROLL,
Alice's Adventures in Wonderland

IT SEEMED TO me that the time between our visit to Dr. de Lotbinière and the day set for Margaret's surgery at WMC in Valhalla would stretch endlessly. I wondered how we would cope over the next twelve days with the suspense and the anxiety, not to speak of the fear that Margaret might die before the surgery if the expanding tumor caused a hemorrhage between now and then. But in fact the next twelve days would turn out to be so busy that we scarcely had time to worry.

Preparing for brain surgery is like setting out for the longest and most challenging of journeys. You make lists, fill out forms, try to decide what to pack and how to deal with everything that will be left behind while on a long voyage the destination of which remains unclear.

Dr. D's patient secretary Bonnie had provided me with a mass of paperwork, as well as a long list of things we must do to prepare for surgery. Perhaps the most reassuring information was that Medicare, plus my secondary coverage, UnitedHealthcare, would pick up about 90 percent of the cost. The financial office of WMC was blissfully vague about what the total would amount to since Medicare would cover most of it, but gentle prodding, aided by a quick scan on the internet, indicated that it would run into the mid–six figures—in fact, the bills for Margaret's first brain surgery would eventually come to about $450,000—leading me to realize how fortunate I was to have made a smooth, indeed effortless transition from the excellent health coverage I had enjoyed for forty-eight years at Simon & Schuster to my retirement and Medicare. Given my Medicare number and that of my secondary insurance, nobody at WMC or in Dr. Alain's office was concerned about my ability to pay for whatever was in store; there were no complications, no anguished telephone calls, no disputes about what was covered and what was not, no red tape or fuss. As the statements began to come in over the months ahead, it was difficult not to wonder how the mere fact of having had a good job and living until the age of sixty-five separated me from the many millions of people for whom this level of medical treatment would either be impossible or lead to bankruptcy. All you had to do was live to the right age and in a part of the country where there is no shortage of good, even great hospitals, to be almost totally covered, whatever happened. I gave silent thanks to President Lyndon B. Johnson, who put through Medicare in 1965, and gets little credit for it, and to those who have kept it intact since then despite efforts to diminish it.

I cleared my desk of its normal clutter and put everything down in some sort of priority, while Margaret went upstairs to her own office, a converted bedroom above my office where she kept the filing cabinets containing her horses' paperwork over the years, and the bulky files for each of the annual Stonegate Cross-Country Schooling Trials, which she had put on for the last twenty-five years. At their peak Margaret had as many as 150 horses and riders competing at three levels—Beginner-Novice,

Novice, and Training—over courses she had designed herself, not to speak of everything that goes with a combined training event: USCTA technical delegate, almost fifty volunteer fence judges with walkie-talkies, a sound system and an announcer, a vet, a blacksmith, an EMT with an ambulance, a caterer, a secretary to check every competitor's entry forms, people to oversee the parking of trucks and horse trailers (and tow them out with a tractor if it got muddy), a starter, and an assistant with an electronic stopwatch to record times—in short, a huge effort that kept her fully occupied all winter. It was also a year-round task to maintain and improve over fifty fences and keep the courses free of rocks or woodchuck holes.

Even in bad weather Margaret hated to be indoors. She was happiest outdoors, walking her land when she was not riding on it—a farmer's daughter, as comfortable in muddy Wellies as in high heels. People who didn't know her well assumed that she spent her time riding or getting herself ready to go out to dinner, without realizing that she was also the chief executive and organizer of a large-scale horse event that took place at the beginning of May every year regardless of weather, required nearly a year of preparation, and always made a profit, or that she regarded her horses, her barn, and every acre of our land as her personal responsibility. When it came to what was hers, Margaret's eye was on the sparrow.

I half-heartedly emailed replies to a few friends who knew that Margaret had been going down to see Dr. de Lotbinière, all variations on the same message: "We have been consulting with brain surgeons, and have chosen one, and Margaret will have surgery on Wednesday next week . . . Of course, time is of the essence, the clock is ticking, but I think we have a very good man, and there is an excellent chance he will remove all the tumor, then we'll see . . ."

I did not add that I was shit-scared.

I assumed Margaret was sending similar messages to her friends upstairs from her cell phone, but after a time I heard what sounded like an electric appliance instead. A Dustbuster, perhaps? But why would Margaret be vacuuming? I left my desk and climbed the steep, narrow staircase to her office, made more challenging by a ninety-degree turn midway—it had not yet occurred to me that she might very soon not be able to get up to it again—to find her at her desk feeding photographs into her paper shredder. There were boxes and thick files full of photographs on the desk, one of them of her first husband Donald Williams in front of her— she always referred to him as "the good-looking one" among her three husbands. "Don *was* good-looking," I said, glancing at it. "Yes, he was," Margaret said, as she slipped his photograph into the shredder with no visible emotion.

Margaret's marriage to Don was something of a mystery. In 1955, at the age of eighteen she graduated from a hum-drum secretarial school in London and made the surprising decision to take a job in Kenya, then still a Crown colony, while the Mau Mau Uprising against British rule was still going on. It was in effect a war zone, as well as a journey of three days and nights from England by air, via Rome, Khartoum, and Entebbe in a twin-engine, propeller-driven aircraft. The job she was going to was that of a secretary in the Criminal Investigation Department of the Royal Kenya Police in Nyeri, a small town in the middle of the heavily forested Aberdare highlands about sixty miles as the crow flies from Nairobi, the heartland of the uprising.

No doubt Margaret had craved something more exciting than a secretarial job at home in England, and her father would surely have encouraged her to find one—Paul Mogford had always regretted not going out to farm in Canada or Australia when he was a young man, so he would have been the last person to hold his daughter back from a colonial adventure.

In Nyeri Margaret shared a cottage on the golf course with another secretary, and carried a Luger pistol in the waistband of her skirt, as well as a boxer on a leash, whenever she went for a walk—not uncommon precautions during the Mau Mau "emergency." The pistol was surely loaned to Margaret by her boss and future husband, the handsome young district police commissioner of Nyeri, who also taught her to shoot it—she would remain an excellent pistol shot until her illness, admired at the Pleasant Valley pistol range for more than her looks.

At what point she and Don Williams became lovers it is impossible to know, but less than a year after her arrival in Kenya they were married at Saint Cuthbert's Church in Nyeri, a full-scale colonial wedding with Margaret in white and Don in dress uniform, photographed as they emerged from the church under crossed swords, with kilted bagpipers in the background, bound for the wedding reception at the famous Outspan Hotel.

They separated less than a year later and Margaret moved for a while to Nairobi, where she exercised the race horses of Beryl Markham, famed aviatrix, author of the beloved aviation classic *West with the Night*, perhaps the last survivor of the wild and wicked days of "White Mischief," the colorful set of hard-drinking, hard-living colonial whites described in Isak Dinesen's *Out of Africa*. (For those who remember the 1985 film based on it, which won the Academy Award for Best Picture, Beryl Markham was the horsey English adolescent who befriends Baroness von Blixen, played by Meryl Streep.)

Margaret only occasionally alluded to her life in Nairobi at the age of twenty, and on the rare occasions when she mentioned her first husband Don she never spoke badly of him, but it was noticeable that while every flat surface in the house was crowded with framed photographs of all the people and animals that had played an important role in her life, including her second husband, Magnum photographer Burt Glinn, Don's photograph was conspicuously missing.

It was in Nyeri that Margaret began a lifelong habit of sunbathing whenever she had the time and the opportunity. The fact that Nyeri is less than ninety miles from the equator and almost six thousand feet high did not seem to her dangerous regarding sun exposure, nor to anyone else at the time. A tan was her definition of glowing health, beauty, and above all glamor, as it was for many women, particularly those coming from a country with a climate like England's. A year-round tan was sexy, it suggested skiing holidays in Switzerland, summers on the Riviera, winter cruises in the Caribbean; it wasn't something you could get at home in the Cotswolds, so for a young woman with a pale English skin it was a kind of transformation. Where other people were careful to wear a hat and a long-sleeved shirt in the tropics, Margaret stripped to the skimpiest two-piece bathing suit she could find or get away with (the bikini had been around since 1946 in France, but it must still have required a certain amount of daring to wear one in colonial Kenya in 1957) and exposed herself to the East African noonday sun blazing down on her fiercely from a cloudless sky, rubbing in a little Johnson's baby oil from time to time to keep her skin from drying out. The sun was her friend, and remarkably she never suffered from sunburn, as I did—her skin turned almost instantly to the exact shade of tan that surfers in Southern California sought. It would not occur to Margaret until it was too late that pursuing the sun might be a fatal addiction.

"I've been having a hard time sending emails from my phone," she said. "My fingers seem worse." She held up her right hand, and showed me that she could no longer touch her fingertips to her palm. "I tried to answer Megan's email, but I couldn't." Megan had worked in Margaret's barn and helped to exercise her horses for nearly twelve years; smart, pretty, and blond, she was something like a surrogate daughter—Margaret had never wanted children of her own but was not without motherly feelings—if she had had a daughter she would have wanted her to be like Megan. Married now, with a daughter of her own, Megan would of course be the first person to whose message Margaret wanted to reply. "So I'm tidying up instead," she went on, sounding, unlike her normal self, ever so slightly helpless.

I did not think it would help matters to ask why one of the things Margaret wanted to tidy up was her first marriage. Besides, a glance at her wastepaper basket showed that it was already full of horsey bits and pieces off her desk, engraved paperweights, framed dressage results, photographs of Margaret jumping big walls and fences on horses long since departed—Margaret never sold a horse, once they were in her barn they stayed for life, looked after just as carefully as they were in their prime even when their days of being ridden were long since gone.

I understood perfectly. Before every big move in her life Margaret liked to make a "clean sweep" of the past with ruthless efficiency, although this time she must have realized the hopelessness of the task as she looked around her at the walls hung with ribbons, hundreds of them, and the glass cabinets full of silver trophies of every shape and form. Even if she devoted the next twelve days to the job she was unlikely to produce a clean slate here.

The thought must have occurred to her too. She picked up her cell phone and made another stab at emailing Megan. Her fingers moved slowly and clumsily, but she finally completed a brief message, sent it off with a swoosh, then burst into tears. "It's never going to get better, is it?" she asked.

Margaret was not a woman who cried easily or for no good

reason, but once she started, it took her some time to stop—then, when the tears were over, she set her jaw and got down to facing what had to be faced. She would not cry again for the next twelve days.

Somewhere in the many notebooks all over the house in which Margaret recorded in a firm bold hand things she had read that captured her attention and that applied to her, she wrote down a sentence by Isak Dinesen: "The cure for anything is salt water—sweat, tears or the sea." It must have made an impact on her, she had carefully underlined it twice.

"You're tired," I said, "it's been a long, hard day. You'll see, things will look better tomorrow."

Margaret dabbed at her face with a Kleenex. "I don't think so," she said.

She was right. The next day was awful. Whether this was or was not a psychosomatic reaction to facing the fact that she was going to have brain surgery, Margaret's symptoms worsened overnight. The fingers of her right hand became even more difficult to use, so much so that it was hard for her to deal with the buttons of her jeans and shirts, or to tie her own shoelaces. At the same time, her lips began to droop ever so slightly on the right side of her face, and chewing became more difficult, as if she were losing control of those muscles. The fact that she could see this for herself every time she looked in a mirror made it seem even more serious to Margaret than the problem with her fingers, but worst of all was the sudden onset of diarrhea, which seemed unconnected to the brain tumor, although it may have been a side effect of her anxiety.

Margaret's bag of pills in the dressing room of her horse trailer always contained Lomotil and Immodium—no serious competitive rider wants to risk having to withdraw from an event because of something he or she might have eaten the night before—but neither of these slowed the diarrhea down a bit. A call to our friend Dr. Tom got Margaret an appointment with Dr. Salvatore Buffa, a genial gastroenterologist in Poughkeepsie, who saw Margaret the next day. He told her this was a fairly common reaction to the contrast fluid she had to drink before the full-body scans the day before. It would take a while for the liquid to work its way out of her system.

Dr. Buffa, a large, bluff, friendly man captured Margaret's confidence immediately—he prescribed something a lot stronger than what she was taking. While Margaret had a fear of doctors, she also had a touching trust in prescriptions. The quickest way to her heart was with a prescription pad; she had the same unquestioning faith in a prescription that Catholics have in the wafer at Holy Communion. Her favorite doctor had been her old friend and internist Mort Shapiro, dead now, alas, who always carried a prescription pad in his pocket—even at black-tie dinners Mort would whip it out if anyone mentioned a symptom, however slight, and scrawl a prescription, saying, "Take these, bubbi, you'll feel better in no time." Mort never hesitated to prescribe opium drops for an upset stomach, major-league painkillers for the slightest headache, or huge quantities of Naproxen for an aching back. What Mort offered, and what Margaret wanted from a doctor, was instant relief, but that was not on offer from Dr. Buffa, who recommended "BRAT," a diet of bananas, rice, applesauce, and toast over the next few days instead.

This was not in itself a problem, Margaret had very little appetite but she quite liked rice and toast. What was more alarming was the rapidly increasing paralysis of her lips and facial muscles, which made everything difficult to eat. It was not just that it became hard for her to chew; the lack of feeling in her lips made her fearful that she was drooling without realizing it. Quite suddenly, even the ordinary, everyday moments of her life made her self-conscious—she needed to use a straw to have morning coffee in the tack room with Megan and Miguel; it was difficult for her to articulate, which made it hard to talk to anyone on the telephone, even close friends; the difficulty of using the fingers of her right hand made answering emails almost impossible. It was as if she had been cut off overnight from the world, at just the point when she most needed support.

The list of things that suddenly became difficult for Margaret grew frighteningly long: doing up her bra, flossing her teeth, using a spoon, making tea, putting on her makeup, fastening a necklace, writing out a shopping list, taking her watch off. It seemed as if every hour brought her face-to-face with something ordinary she could no longer do. I did my best to help, but my fingers were often clumsy, which made her ever more irritated not to be able to do these simple, everyday things.

On the one hand, she was anxious about the surgery; on the other, she wanted to hurry up and get it over with in the hope that she would be able to resume a normal life afterward. References to "quality of life" from a doctor, even the sympathetic Dr. Alain, only increased her anxiety. For to her that phrase meant riding her horses, driving her car, going out to dinner with friends, and now it seemed to be narrowing down to closing the zipper of her jeans or fastening the hooks of her bra.

Every day seemed to present some new health problem, as if Margaret were being made to pay day by day for all those years of robust health and physical activity. The day after seeing Dr. Buffa, Margaret had an attack of cystitis, one of those things that happened to her from time to time for no apparent reason and for which she kept a supply of Bactrim in the bag of pills in the dressing room of her trailer, just in case that should occur when she was competing. Cystitis was no big deal for her—it's one of those complaints that men don't suffer from and therefore tend to dismiss as a "woman's problem"—but this time the cystitis grew more and more severe with frightening speed, and combined with the diarrhea and her anxiety it turned Margaret into what she most feared to be, sickly, an invalid, a *patient*, in constant need of cleaning and care. Her gynecologist was in Manhattan, a two-hour drive away, as was her internist, but I could see during the night that she was getting sicker by the hour: her face was alarmingly pale, she had a fever, her hands were trembling badly. I bundled her up into the car in the morning over her increasingly faint objections and took her to the ER at the Vassar Brothers Medical Center in Poughkeepsie, fortunately at a moment when there were no victims of gunshot wounds, a heart attack, or a car crash waiting; in fact, we had the waiting room pretty much to ourselves.

"I don't want to stay here," she whispered to me, but the ER doctor's instant diagnosis that Margaret was suffering from an acute urinary tract infection and severe dehydration, combined with his firm but gentle manner—he seemed to me absurdly young, but already endowed with a great bedside manner—calmed her at once. She needed to have sodium chloride and an antibiotic administered intravenously, he explained. Margaret handed me her handbag and sweater and lay down obediently. She was better at dealing with a medical problem after it had been named and a solution proposed to her. Once she knew what was going to be done and why, she could be a model patient. An authoritative diagnosis lifted her spirits almost as much as a prescription. It was the unknown she disliked.

As a child, Margaret had been sent to a boarding school run by nuns—her parents were not Catholic, but, like many middle-class English people at the time, they believed that the nuns were better at teaching and disciplining girls, that a convent school was a step up socially and academically. Margaret had hated being sent away to school; her experience at the hands of the nuns who enforced discipline with a briskly wielded ruler or cane gave her a lifelong hostility toward the Catholic Church and its teachings— to the end of her life she still wondered from time to time how her father and mother could have been so cruel as to send her away when everything she loved, pony, dog, and cats, was at home. That her father simply thought it was the best thing he could do for her she never accepted.

Much as Margaret had hated the nuns at the convent, she regarded the priest paradoxically as an authority figure, with even more power than the Mother Superior. The priest could be appealed to, he could overrule Mother Superior and allow Margaret to go home for the weekend if she had misbehaved. As an adult she projected these feelings onto doctors: they too were authority figures, they had the wherewithal to ease pain, tell her what the problem was, and deal with it. She did not exactly *trust* them, but she acknowledged with whatever reluctance their power.

Over the next year we would become reluctant connoisseurs of emergency rooms, and while the one at Vassar Brothers was not at the top of our list, lying there in the examination room with the intravenous needles in her arm and the lights turned down seemed to bring Margaret to a kind of peace that she had not felt since her diagnosis. The small room was decorated in various shades of green, the kind of colors you only see in a hospital, but it was quiet, and as the transparent plastic pouches slowly drained into her arm, Margaret began to look more like herself, not quite asleep but restful and composed, with some color returning to her face. Being in the ER removed her for a time from the decisions we had to make, it was a moment of escape; ironically, she would look back on this as one of her best moments in the days to come.

The cystitis ebbed and by the next day it was under control, but the diarrhea continued. Other things were becoming more difficult. Even the most ordinary household tasks. Although Margaret did not exactly *like* doing laundry (who does?), she had exacting standards about how it should be done, and found a certain peace in carefully folding it and putting it away. Her mother Kit—she always addressed her parents as Paul and Kit, and as far as I could tell always had—was a wonderful cook and a perfectionist housekeeper, and Kit somehow managed to pass this on to her daughter, a vast multigenerational knowledge of how to cook, clean, and put away anything. Margaret would become a world traveler and a model at an early age, but in some corner of her mind she was also her mother's daughter. Ironing pleats perfectly, preparing a crown roast of lamb, folding laundry neatly and putting it away in exact piles, these were all hardwired into Margaret, she was happy to leave the tasks to somebody else, but she was no more likely to miss a fingerprint on a glass or to serve ready-made mint sauce from a bottle instead of making it from scratch than Kit had been.

The next day was devoted to "pre-op" tests at Westchester Medical Center in Valhalla, New York, where the surgery would take place. Unlike the soothing ambience and décor of the Northern Westchester Cancer Treatment and Wellness Center, WMC is a big, intimidating hospital, a sprawling, formidable presence that dominates the small and oddly named town of Valhalla, with over six hundred beds and nine hundred consulting physicians, on a campus it shares with the New York State Police and the Westchester County Jail, a pretty grim landscape viewed from one of the many parking lots. WMC serves the Hudson Valley region as well as northern New Jersey and southern Connecticut, and like a lot of major hospitals it is in a more or less constant process of rebuilding and expansion, so that it's almost impossible to get to any part of it in a direct line; instead one passes constantly from a run-down, old-fashioned area to a stunningly modern one, guided by temporary signs that seem to lead you nowhere, after a long walk that often brings you back to the place you started from, asking for directions for the second or third time from harried doctors and nurses. The lobby was serene and sleek, like the departure lounge of a modern airport, except that here we were taking a journey of undetermined duration into the unknown. Big hospitals are impersonal, frightening places, phenomenally busy. Especially for someone who has never been a patient in one, it's easy to feel one is on a conveyor belt. WMC was no exception.

The waiting room to the Radiology Department was all bare wood and sleek plastic furniture, rather like a Scandinavian sauna. Margaret went off to undress and put on a hospital gown, leaving me with her handbag to sit and listen to people exchanging horror stories about their cancer treatment or unimaginable injuries. I had negotiated with numerous emails and telephone calls for the use of a contrast fluid that would not worsen Margaret's diarrhea. Once radiologists listened to the problem, they said, oh, sure, of course there was an alternative. Then why not use one that didn't cause the problem in the first place? I couldn't help thinking.

I also had a pocketful of Margaret's jewelry. She did not own anything in the way of valuable jewelry, always preferring a new horse or a saddle to a bracelet or a necklace, but she never took off her wedding ring, or the engagement ring I had bought because neither of her two previous husbands had bought her one. Even more important to her was the gold Cartier "Love Bracelet" I had bought her in 1976, when we were first living together. In those days Cartier had a policy that you couldn't buy one for yourself.

You had to go to Cartier with the person who was buying it for you, and sit while the bracelet was fastened around your wrist with tiny gold screws using the gold screwdriver that came with the bracelet. The whole idea was that you wore it for life; Cartier made something of a small ceremony of it. That day in 1976, we had lunch, drank a toast to our new state, then walked back to Fifth Avenue—I was going back to my office in Rockefeller Center. As we passed Cartier I told her there was something I wanted to show her, and led her upstairs to the department, where we were seated quickly and they fastened the bracelet on. "I will always wear it," Margaret said, to gentle applause from everyone in the service department. That was the whole idea, of course, you wore it for life, at Cartier they screwed it on tightly with that in mind. Removing it for the MRI not only challenged my eyesight and dexterity, but deeply upset Margaret. She had worn it for almost forty years through thick and thin, and taking it off seemed to her a surrender to the unthinkable.

Most people who do dangerous things are superstitious. Margaret never competed without her "lucky coin," a ten-dollar gold piece; a four-leaf clover she had found in our fields and preserved in Scotch tape; and her rings and bracelet. She had never had a serious injury, and mostly won, so perhaps they worked. I knew how vulnerable she must feel without her "things," as she called them, and how scared she was that she would never put them on again—in fact she wouldn't, when her world began to revolve around a regular MRI. But all that was thankfully in the future on April 12, 2016, as Margaret took the all-important brain scan that would guide Dr. Alain in his surgery on April 20.

About an hour later Margaret appeared, fully dressed again, to reclaim her handbag and her jewelry. Her face was strained—the care and precision with which the brain scan was taken were enough to emphasize how serious her surgery would be. "Let's get out of here," she said. She sat upright and silent in the car on the way home, staring at the road ahead. Whatever was on her mind, she did not want to discuss it in front of Rob Tyson, our friend and driver now that cataracts prevented me from driving any farther than our local supermarket or to the Dunkin' Donuts for morning coffee, but when we got out of the car she felt for the missing bracelet and said, "My whole world is unraveling," then went indoors to put together a late lunch for both of us.

❧

I listened to the telephone messages, including one from Dr. Alain's secretary Bonnie to call her as soon as possible. I did so at once. She had forgotten to tell us, she said, that Margaret would need a physical examination to certify that she was fit for surgery. I gave a small, silent sigh. Margaret liked her internist Dr. Adam Rosenblüth, but the last thing she wanted at this point was to drive down to New York City to see him—her patience with doctors, never infinite, was coming to an end. Still, after I explained what was needed, she bit the bullet and I made an appointment with "Dr. Adam" (his father, "Dr. Michael," was my internist, and they shared an office) for the day after tomorrow. As it turned out, the visit was short, sympathetic, and to the point. Margaret was that rare person of seventy-eight who was 100 percent physically fit except for the tumor that was trying to kill her—apart from that Dr. Adam could find nothing wrong with her. He too thought that she would benefit from going somewhere for rehabilitation after the surgery, but I could see from the set of her jaw that she didn't want to hear about it. Dr. Adam and I exchanged significant looks as Margaret got dressed, meaning *one step at a time*, and I made a mental note to talk to her neurosurgeon Dr. Alain about this.

❧

I realized that I had not given enough thought to what Margaret would, or more important would *not*, be able to do once she was discharged from the hospital. We lived in a big eighteenth century house, about the many inconveniences of which I had written a whole book, *Country Matters*. Would she be able to get up and down the stairs, or to use the old-fashioned bathtubs? To what extent would she be handicapped, and for how long? When I returned home from Johns Hopkins after prostate cancer surgery over two decades ago I had a nurse for some time, a burly former paratroop medic named Emory who had helped me bathe, dress, and exercise, looked after my catheter bag, and was invariably cheerful and optimistic. As military veterans (he of the Eighty-Second Airborne, me of the Royal Air Force) Emory and I had bonded instantly. Would Margaret need someone similar? But Margaret was adamant, she did not want a stranger living in the house.

Margaret had already asked Megan's mother, Colleen Sinon, a neighbor, friend, and licensed practical nurse, to come over and tell her what she needed to take with her to the hospital. Staring at a yellow legal pad and trying to imagine what she might find useful or necessary for a long stay in hospital had not so far produced anything helpful. The list was either too short or seemed endlessly long, as if Margaret were trying to pack for a cruise. In her previous marriage, to Burt Glinn, she had traveled all over the world to places unimaginably remote and difficult, so she was of necessity a disciplined and well-organized packer, but this was not a trip during which she would be expected to look her best, or style her own hair.

It was clear she was not going to need makeup, nightgowns, or even a hairbrush. It was more a question of what she needed to leave behind, as Colleen explained when she came over for a drink on Friday. She would not need her cell phone, or an alarm clock, or even her watch, still less the collapsible Brot magnifying makeup mirror without which Margaret never went anywhere, even to horse events where she got up before dawn to compete, or to tented camps in Tanzania where they brought you a cup of tea, two biscuits, and a lantern in the dark so you could get out on safari as the sun was rising.

Basically, everything Margaret needed would be provided by the hospital, anything else that she found she wanted I could bring from home since I would be visiting her every day. Margaret looked a little skeptical at this—she did not rate my ability to find exactly the item she wanted very highly—but over drinks we cut down the list to what she regarded as the bare essentials. At least half a dozen ChapSticks—Margaret always carried one in her purse, scattered them throughout the house, had several in the car, she was never without one, even on horseback in competition. If she found herself without a ChapStick it was necessary to get one at once, the absence of a ChapStick was one of the few things that made her panic. She would need her four-leaf clover, her own slippers, Clinique face moisturizer, toothbrush, toothpaste, handkerchiefs, dressing gown, and underwear. I could see from the expression on Colleen's face that much of this was not going to prove useful, but at the same time I thought Margaret would feel better knowing that she had it all with her in the Vuitton tote bag that had accompanied her around the world.

Colleen too thought that Margaret might need some rehabilitation before she came home, but she was too tactful to press that to the point of spooking Margaret. She was confident that nurses could be found locally if needed, and spoke highly of the outpatient rehabilitation services of MidHudson Hospital in Poughkeepsie, where she had worked as a nurse for many years. I tucked this in the back of my mind. Among her many skills, Colleen was good at calming Margaret's anxiety—it wasn't merely a technique, there was a genuine affection between the two of them. Margaret would listen to Colleen without any of the skepticism she felt about doctors. Colleen was an attractive woman, sympathetic, full of practical advice, and although both a mother and motherly, which Margaret was not, she lived surrounded by her own shifting cloud of animals, dogs, cats, ponies, horses, and miniature donkeys; in fact, we had first met her shortly after we moved to the country when her father turned up early one morning looking for one of her missing ponies, which, it turned out, had managed to cross two busy roads and walk a mile to graze on our property. Whether it was Colleen's presence or not, Margaret seemed to relax a bit after she had completed the list of what needed to be packed. At least she had a plan.

For the next few days we had glorious spring weather, perfect for riding, the kind we'd had in mind when we bought the house in Dutchess County, not as yet having experienced the March nor'easters which dump vast quantities of wet snow and bring down the trees and power lines, or the bugs, humidity, and sullen thunder of August. Margaret rode her horses in the sun, determined not to show any signs of fear or anxiety to "her people." In my spare time I cruised the internet, reading up on brain surgery and rehabilitation as if I were going to be examined on the subjects, while she went through her riding routine. Did she want to imprint in her mind every jump, every foot of the trails on which she rode her horses, all the things she loved doing, and the small world she had made for herself? She had created it step by step over the years, it was like a magic kingdom, a perfect place to ride her horses, and she must have wondered if she would ever ride over it again. She had the kind of eerie calm that comes over people—I had seen it in the Royal Air Force—who are about to make their first parachute jump, when it is too late to back out of it and there is nothing left but to throw oneself out the open door into space and hope for the best.

Behind the calm, however, things were not going well for her as the date for surgery approached. In fact, things were bad enough for me to email Dr. Alain about my concerns. "Margaret's ability to speak has deteriorated very sharply over the past 24 hours, also her ability to use her fingers . . . Her diarrhea symptoms have diminished, but she is still hampered by great (and increasing) difficulty to chew and swallow. Lips, facial muscles, etc., all worsening."

Dr. Alain was swiftly reassuring on all these subjects. The worsening symptoms were to be expected as the tumor continued to put pressure on her brain. I did my best to pass these reassurances on to Margaret, who by this time just wanted to get it over with.

4.

MARGARET DIDN'T SAY much on the way down to Westchester Medical Center at dawn on Wednesday, April 20, 2016. We had been up at five a.m. for a six o'clock departure, the day already seeming endless before it had even begun. She wore her biggest, darkest sunglasses, her "Audrey Hepburn sunglasses," I called them, and which I reminded myself I would have to take home with me. The reality that Margaret would *not* be coming home with me was beginning to sink in. As we pulled into the parking lot she said, "I hope I have everything I need."

"You have everything on the list." Her bag seemed to weigh a ton, despite Colleen's efforts to pare the list down.

"I don't have my wallet." Margaret's wallet was one of those big leather ones that fold over, and it contained a lot more than bills and change. It weighed down her handbag like a brick. Some people's wallet is a thin case for bills, credit cards, and driver's license, but Margaret's practically defined her, it contained almost everything that was important to her. She carried an astonishing weight in quarters and pennies alone—she liked to have on hand a good supply of quarters for places where you can't get a shopping cart without inserting one, the pennies I have no idea what for. Also included: a gold-plated "New York Veteran Police" shield, a gift from one of our dearest friends when he retired from the NYPD as a deputy inspector; good-luck charms of every kind acquired over the years; photographs of me and of her favorite cats and horses; a formidable number of keys on a heavy silver key chain; an emergency key for her car; credit cards; a thick sheaf of membership cards for everything from the AARP to the United States Eventing Association; small pieces of paper with lines from her favorite poems; and a London bobby's police whistle. Leaving it all behind must have felt to her like being naked in the street. Colleen had been adamant, however, that she was to take nothing valuable or irreplaceable with her to hospital. Margaret could see the logic of that. After all, she wasn't going to need money or credit cards, and there wouldn't be any place to lock it all up, so I had put her leopard-print handbag and her wallet in her closet, where she could retrieve them when she returned home, but she didn't feel good about it. Neither did I.

You always imagine there will be more time to talk things over, until there isn't. I had thought the admissions process would be long and complicated, but in the computer age this is no longer necessarily so, at any rate not at WMC. All the paperwork had been done electronically by Bonnie, so in minutes we were upstairs, Margaret had changed into a hospital gown, and she was lying motionless in a narrow curtained-off space, still wearing her sunglasses. Her stoicism in the face of serious adversity was on display; it was the small things in life that drove her crazy, not the big ones. I stuffed her clothes and shoes into my bag, which was already heavy enough—we had been told the surgery would take at least four hours, so I had brought down my laptop and a thick batch of files to keep me busy while I waited.

Margaret, I noticed, elicited a certain amount of curiosity among the nurses, which at first I attributed to her sunglasses until it dawned on me that the brain surgery Dr. Alain was about to perform was a big deal, high up on the list of the most difficult, precise, and complex procedures one can undergo. Margaret was the star of the day, medically speaking. She was given a tranquilizer and had a brief talk with her anesthesiologist, who seemed absurdly young for such a serious responsibility, and who like all anesthesiologists promised her she would feel nothing. Then there followed a long wait, so long that I wondered if something had gone wrong, then at last Dr. Alain arrived, again faultlessly dressed in street clothes, to apologize for the delay. The previous surgery had taken longer than anticipated, the operating room was being prepared for him now, he would begin shortly.

There was a brief flurry of activity. One of Dr. Alain's assistants arrived with a consent form and a pen, a nurse put an IV into Margaret's wrist. Margaret finally handed her sunglasses to me—there were no tears in her eyes—and I kissed her forehead, which was as cold as ice, and squeezed her hand. "Don't forget to feed the cats," she said, then she was gone.

I had some paperwork to bring to the hospital accounting office, so I took the elevator down to the basement, set off carrying Margaret's tote bag and my own, and promptly got lost. I circled endlessly, weighed down like a donkey, for what felt like miles. It was as if I were trapped in a maze; some corridors ended in a blank wall, others ended at locked doors with signs that read "No Entry" and warned of contagious diseases or radiation. This was the working part of the hospital, no windows, not a place for visitors. There was almost nobody around, and those few I encountered either had no idea where accounting was or told me to turn around and go back to where I had started from, which I couldn't find.

It was like a labyrinth; the legend of Theseus and Ariadne's ball of string came to my mind. There were several different banks of elevators, and by the time I had completed my errand and finally gotten back to the right floor again I was no longer sure which of the many surgical waiting rooms I had been told to sit in. Nothing looked familiar, I did not even recognize the place where Margaret and I had been waiting earlier, still less any of the nurses, none of whom in any case seemed to know in which operating theater Dr. de Lotbinière was performing surgery. There was a desk and telephone in each of the waiting rooms but they were all empty. There was nobody to ask, so I picked a room at random, hoping Dr. Alain would find me there.

By now I had worked myself into a state of acute anxiety. How would Dr. Alain find me? What if I were needed for some reason? I thought of calling Bonnie in his office, but I wasn't getting a cell phone signal, for some reason. I had experienced a sudden panic attack like this some years ago the night before I was going down to Johns Hopkins in Baltimore early in the morning for cancer surgery. I became convinced that I had lost our airline tickets, I was unable to find them anywhere in the house, and I experienced a full-blown panic attack, covered in sweat, struggling for breath, heartbeat surging out of control, I was ripping open envelopes, dumping the contents of my bag on the floor, shouting at the top of my voice. Margaret had succeeded in calming me down, and we eventually found the tickets just where I had carefully put them, on the hall table.

I had recognized then, and some part of my mind recognized now, that what I was doing was transferring anxiety about the impending surgery, then mine, now hers, onto an inconsequential or imaginary problem. The tickets could have been replaced at the airport when we checked in, Dr. Alain or one of the nurses would surely find me sooner or later wherever I sat, but panic, like terror, is beyond reason. Perhaps an irrational burst of panic at things that *don't* matter is the price of remaining calm about the things that do, a compensatory mechanism for the fabled

English stiff upper lip. The English pride themselves above all on not displaying emotion or fear in difficult situations, no tears, no sobs, no lamentations, "Keep calm and carry on" may be the unofficial national motto, but no doubt it comes at a cost. Anxiety is bound to emerge somewhere, like water from a hidden leak, but this time I didn't have Margaret to calm me down.

I sat down, took a sip of water, and regained control of myself. Many hours seemed to have passed, but when I looked at my watch I was startled to see that it was only half an hour since I had said goodbye to Margaret. The surgery would probably not even have begun yet.

I didn't want to risk getting hopelessly lost again, so I decided not to set off in search of the cafeteria. I had a granola bar and a bottle of water in my bag, and that would have to do. As I tried to read what I had brought with me, I found myself wishing that I had not watched Dr. Brett Osborn's video of himself performing a craniotomy. I could remember only too clearly what it looked like, but this time the patient was not a stranger whose face one never sees, but Margaret. Only a year and a half later, when I read Dr. Alain's "Operative Report" on the "Left-sided frontoparietal MRI-guided stereotactic craniotomy for resection of tumor," dictated after performing the surgery, did I fully realize what was involved. Margaret was "placed under general anesthesia . . . following a smooth, atraumatic intubation, electrodes were attached for the purposes of monitoring somatosensory evoked potentials and motor evoked responses . . . an arterial line was them inserted along with a Foley catheter following which the Mayfield head tongs were applied to the patient's skull . . . The position of the incision was mapped out onto the skin of the patient and a small amount of hair clipped in the adjacent territory." Alain clearly kept his promise to Margaret about her hair.

He then made an incision in Margaret's scalp, peeled back the skin and the muscle from the cheekbone to the top of the skull in exactly the arc he had traced on her head with his finger when he first saw her in his office, marked the position of the tumor on the skull as determined by her most recent MRI, and performed "a generous craniotomy." The bone flap was set aside and the dura mater, the membrane enclosing the brain, was exposed, revealing "an expanded gyrus immediately underneath the center of the craniotomy," in other words a raised place or bump in the dura at the point where the tumor rose toward the surface of the brain. This too reconfirmed Alain's diagnosis on reviewing Margaret's first MRI: "Fortunately for the patient, the tumor comes to within a few millimeters of the cortex," he had written, meaning that "relatively little normal brain tissue would need to be sacrificed in order to remove the tumor . . ." The closer the tumor is to the surface of the brain, the easier it is to reach, of course, and the less brain tissue would have to be removed to get at it. Alain then performed a cross-shaped incision in the dura and folded it back toward the edges, exposing the brain.

It is hard to do justice to the delicacy and precision of the surgery Dr. Alain was performing. At this point he mapped out the surface of the brain and decided how to approach the tumor. The microscope was brought up, he incised the delicate pia-arachnoid "with micro scissors" then the sulcus was "splayed apart using gentle traction."

Despite the even tenor of the Operative Report, one can sense at this point a certain satisfaction at having reached, so to speak, the heart of the matter, perhaps even a certain awe at gently manipulating the human brain, of all the organs the most complex and mysterious. At the base of the sulcus, a tiny trough between two ridges, he made a small opening into the underlying brain. "A millimeter or two [from] the opening, dark fluid was noted to erupt consistent with hemorrhagic fluid within the tumor." Here was the "necrosis around the tumor," which the neurologist in Poughkeepsie had pointed out to us, the blood and dead matter that the tumor created as it made room for itself inside the brain—a metastatic brain tumor is like a bullet, it cuts its own channel through the brain tissue, more slowly, of course, but with equally devastating effect. "The opening was then enlarged underneath the microscope and small cottonoid patties inserted over at the edge of the corticoid ribbon to protect it. A combination of bipolar cautery and suction was . . . utilized to remove the bulk of the tumor" and specimens were taken for analysis, "the results coming back as . . . consistent with melanoma . . .

"Once the debulking [had] been achieved, the rim of the tumor was gently peeled away from the adjacent brain tissue . . . careful inspection failed to reveal any residual tumor." Dr. Alain irrigated the area, sewed up the layers he had incised, replaced the bone flap "using cranial plates and screws," sewed up the scalp, removed the cranial head tongs, then "a full head dressing" was applied.

The surgery was completed in almost exactly the four hours he had mentioned.

Sitting alone in the waiting room, I plowed through accumulated mail and started in on some of the material I had printed out for myself about metastatic melanoma brain tumors, perhaps not the wisest choice of reading material in the circumstances. I had Googled a lot of pieces on the subject, more than I really wanted, the way a trawler indiscriminately brings a whole lot of fish to the surface in its net, not all of which are worth keeping. Most of my reading these days was about MM (as metastatic melanoma is referred to by many of the doctors). One of the side effects of cancer—I had experienced it at the time of my own two cancer surgeries—is the inability to focus on anything else. In the few days since Margaret's diagnosis I had lost the ability to enjoy reading fiction, or any interest in nonfiction, and given up making a small daily ceremony out of reading every section of the *New York Times* except Sports, even the letters to the editor and the obituaries. Magazines piled up, television series we both enjoyed and normally never missed went unwatched, cancer filled up our lives. Cancer does that; it not only attempts to take over the body, it attempts to take over life, and very often succeeds.

Most of what I was reading did not tell me more about Margaret's brain tumor than I already knew. Some of the personal stories from patients or their loved ones were distressing, and few of them had a happy ending. The importance of speech and physical therapy after surgery was a frequent subject, and I made a note to ask Colleen whether I could arrange for therapy at home once Margaret was discharged from the hospital. A sentence in one of the more academic sites, *Journal of Medicine and Life*, caught my attention sharply. "The prognosis of patients with metastatic malignant melanoma is grim." This was the equivalent of a blow to the solar plexus. It appeared at the very beginning of an article titled "Survival Rates of Patients with Metastatic Malignant Melanoma" cowritten by several oncologists in the flat tones of a scientific paper, and was basically statistical. I read on, with a sick feeling in the pit of my stomach. This was information I did not want to have, presented in its coldest and most mathematical form.

Mark Twain remarked that there are "lies, damned lies and statistics" (he may have borrowed the phrase from Benjamin Disraeli), but these spoke for themselves loud and clear. Of patients who had a complete surgical resection of a skin melanoma in the survey, only 23 percent were alive five years after the excision.

The "lentigo maligna melanoma" on Margaret's right cheek had been excised almost exactly five years ago, so in one sense she was lucky to have survived for so long without any indication of metastases elsewhere in the body. Had the surgeon who excised the melanoma on her face so skillfully been overconfident when she told us that she got it all? Should she have advised us that Margaret should have a PET scan every year just to be on the safe side? An even worse question: *Should we have thought about it ourselves?* The answer was, yes, of course we should have, but Margaret had lived through the five years since that surgery fit, active, without symptoms or health problems of any kind. There had been no reason to suppose that melanoma was metastasizing slowly, insidiously in her body, or, to quote from the survey, that "40.5% of the patients [who had surgery for a 'cutaneous MM'] developed metastases in different organs, especially the brain." Reading on, I noted that an "MM patient with brain metastasis had a risk of dying from this disease about 7 fold higher" than elsewhere in the body and that "metastatic MM has a dismal prognosis with a high mortality rate." The article ended with the flat statement that "the current treatment of brain metastasis is not satisfactory anywhere in the world."

The next article I picked up, this one from the Mayo Clinic, suggested that "complementary treatments" for brain tumor, by which they meant when all else had failed, might include acupuncture, art therapy, exercise, meditation, and music therapy. I did not think that Margaret was likely to take up meditation, still less art or music therapy, under any circumstances. She would want to resume the life she knew, and her first instinct would be to fight hard for it. The Mayo Clinic, however, also emphasized the importance of physical, occupational, and speech therapy in rehabilitation following brain surgery, and recommended that the patient "find a good listener who is willing to listen to you talk about your hopes and fears."

Easier said than done, I thought. Margaret was not someone who would necessarily want to talk to anybody about her hopes and fears. The only friend who had been close enough to her for that was poor Mayo Loiseau Gray, something of a kindred spirit, who for a variety of reasons had run out of hope and killed herself about thirty years ago. Margaret was made of sterner stuff, although she too had moments of depression, loneliness, and despair even when she was well, sudden descents into the depths from which it was difficult to rise. She was kept from sinking like Mayo by physical activity, the sense of command and freedom she felt on a horse, and by her love of animals—taped to the window frame in front of her desk was a treasured piece of paper with some lines by the American nature writer Henry Beston: "For the animal shall not be measured by man, in a world older and more complete than ours they move finished and complete . . . They are not brethren, they are not underlings, they are other nations, caught with ourselves in the net of life and time." This was as near to a system of belief as Margaret had, and not, I thought, a bad one.

In the drab waiting room of WMC—the vast scheme of redecoration at the hospital had not yet reached it—I had suddenly the fear that Margaret and I were to some degree "other nations," as perhaps we all are, and that I might not be the "good listener" the Mayo Clinic had in mind. She had often complained that I did not listen to her, or more precisely that I did not hear what I didn't want to hear. After all, what woman has ever *not* thought this about the man in her life? On reflection I had to admit that she was right. Whatever else I did, I would have to start listening, we were not people with large families, there were just the two of us, we had nobody to fall back on except ourselves.

As if to emphasize this point, large families appeared from time to time in the waiting room: a big Hispanic family with many children, the older women dabbing their eyes with a handkerchief and crossing themselves, speaking in hushed whispers; an Asian family, which had brought along bags full of food in plastic containers, plates, and even a tablecloth and napkins for a full meal; a Russian family of immensely fat men in skintight shorts, the women with handbags big enough to contain a bowling ball. All of these groups left quickly one after the other, either because they were in the wrong waiting room or when they were summoned by a nurse, leaving me alone with my granola bar and my reading material. Whatever surgery a member of their family was undergoing, it was not taking as long as Margaret's; they came and went, I stayed. I felt sure that they would be there to take turns looking after the patient and listening to him or her, that was what families were for, push come to shove, but we had no such resource. We had always imagined we could handle everything by ourselves. I was beginning to have grave doubts about that.

I continued to read, until my eye caught a note somewhere that "occupational therapy" should include the patient's learning to eat again with a knife, fork, and spoon, and that the occupational therapist should provide specially shaped utensils with padded handles to enable the patient to practice using them in conditions that were as realistic as possible. It took a while for this to sink in. The notion that a person recovering from brain surgery might have to learn how to hold a spoon—a *special* spoon, not even an ordinary one—had not occurred to me, nor I was sure, to Margaret.

The whole subject of rehabilitation was obviously going to present more difficulties than I had supposed. If Margaret had to learn to eat all over again, what else would she need to learn?

Our house is full of stairs—would she be able to go up and down them? I made a mental note that we might need more handholds in the bathroom, perhaps even a stair lift? How long would it be before Margaret could drive again? A more sobering question: *Would* she be able to drive again? How long before she could mount a horse? Or wash her hair? Or put on makeup? Or make a cup of tea? (Being English, we don't use tea bags.) Our minds had been focused on the immediate future—the surgery—not on what life would be like *after* surgery. The more I read about rehabilitation, the more questions I had. I would have to find someone who could answer them, and quickly.

The waiting room began to seem like a lonesome place as the afternoon wore on and it emptied out, leaving me alone. For some reason the room seemed darker, but perhaps it was just my mood. Just after five o'clock there was a certain noticeable buzz in the hall outside, nurses springing out of their chairs, the kind of thing that you see in the armed services at the approach of a senior officer, people suddenly looking busy and checking their uniforms. This, as I should have guessed, heralded the approach of Dr. Alain. Unlike many surgeons, he did not appear in his scrubs, but instead wore a tie and a freshly pressed white coat. He sat down beside me and put one hand on my shoulder.

"It's good news," he said. "We removed the tumor."

"Will she be all right?"

He nodded, his expression ever so slightly cautious, that of a man who had learned by experience not to promise more than he could deliver. He meant, I realized later, that she was all right *now*, she had survived the surgery, there would be radiation to come and much else besides, with brain surgery for a metastatic melanoma there could be no guarantee. We chatted briefly, the surgery had gone smoothly, just as planned, she was in good hands. I asked if I could see her. Not yet, he said, she was being moved to the Neuro Intensive Care Unit, I should wait there until one of the nurses brought me in to see her.

It might be some time, he warned.

~◯

The Neuro-ICU was a long way away, back down to the ground floor, then on through many unmarked turns and passages to another bank of elevators that lifted me to a different world. Here, there was a hushed silence, no press of visitors, big double doors that swung closed automatically with a pneumatic swoosh. I asked if I could see Margaret, and was told that a nurse would come out for me eventually—I was to be patient, it would be some time. Behind the reception desk there was a big white plastic board with the names and the medical status of a dozen or so patients. Margaret's name had not yet been added to it.

Margaret had been concerned about whether or not she would be able to have a private room in the hospital. She had a strong sense of privacy, and would not have been comfortable sharing her helplessness with a stranger, but this proved difficult to arrange. No matter how many times I had talked to the admissions office, it was impossible to get a guarantee, it was on an if-and-when basis, Margaret would get a private room *if* one was available *when* she needed it, and that was that. Knowing how strongly Margaret felt about this, I nerved myself up to ask Dr. Alain if he could intervene on her behalf—I don't normally like to pester busy people for small favors—and he told me not to worry, so I assumed it had been taken care of.

Now, in my brief glimpse of the Neuro-ICU, I saw why. Each patient had his or her own "single-occupancy" room, starkly modern and futuristically designed, painted in white and soothing, muted earth tones, with a closed-circuit camera above the bed and a video system to monitor the patient. One wall of the room was a glassed-in booth so that the nurse on duty could keep the patient in view at all times while sitting at his or her desk and computer monitor in the hallway—one nurse to a patient. Above the bed there was a swinging overhead light like that of an operating room, a towering bank of monitors, screens and computers showing a mass of illuminated graphs and flashing numbers next to the bed, and a two-way-mirror flat-screen television set into the wall facing the bed. A large window to the left of the bed gave a view of the rolling green hills of Westchester County. It would be hard to imagine anything more private than this.

At the far end of the hallway was a desk almost the width of the building behind which a mass of screens and monitors blinked and flashed. The only sounds were the occasional muffled ring of a bell and the hum of the air-conditioning system. It was like being on a spaceship. I was reminded of Stanley Kubrick's *2001: A Space Odyssey*, but without the music. If I had not already known how serious the surgery was, the sight of the Neuro-ICU would have told me all I needed to know.

The waiting room here was smaller and cozier than the previous one, with a sofa and a coffee table—I would become familiar with every inch of it over the next few days—and two bathrooms, so there was no need to wander down the hall looking for one. Since I was alone, I found the mute button on the TV remote to silence it and sat down to wait. In about half an hour a large, cheerful, bearded man, looking somewhat like Santa Claus in nurse's scrubs came in. "Margaret's husband?" he asked.

I said I was. He was Margaret's day nurse, and he instantly communicated a rare combination of total commitment and caring. People constantly complain about the impersonality of the medical system, and there is some truth to that as it undergoes a transition to ever larger medical groups and hospital conglomerates on a huge scale, but at what is called in the British armed services "the sharp end of the stick," where actual hands-on patient care takes place, it is constantly amazing how much people *care*.

"You can see her now," he said.

I asked if she had said anything. A few words, he said—it would take some time before the effects of the anesthesia wore off, her speech was not yet clear. I should not expect too much at this point.

I gathered up my things—*our* things—and followed him through the double doors, and past his glassed-in cubbyhole desk into Margaret's room. The floor was littered with the debris of emergency medical care, it is only when the patent is stable and recovering that everything is neat and tidy, when serious things are going on, doctors and nurses rip open the sterilized plastic packages and pouches that contain instruments, tubes, needles, and dressings and drop them on the floor, there isn't time for tidiness. The blinds were partly drawn, so the room was like an aquarium lit by flashing lights and graphs from innumerable monitors. Margaret seemed dwarfed in it by the banks of instruments towering on each side of her bed, her head was covered with what looked like a white eighteenth century Turkish turban shaped like a giant Hershey's Kiss, tubes ran in and out of her, she looked tiny and heartbreakingly fragile, not at all like the person I knew. He drew up a chair for me, I sat down and put my hand in hers. There was no squeeze of recognition on her part. Her eyes were closed.

"She knows you're here," he said softly, then he looked over all the instruments and monitors, made a few adjustments, and withdrew to his glass booth, from which he could keep an eye on things. Apart from her gentle breathing, there was no sign of life from Margaret except the slow drip of innumerable plastic bags into the IV in her wrist, and the even slower drip from her catheter into another plastic bag hanging from the bed. We sat like that for a very long time, until I was worried that I might have to leave at the end of visiting hours before she spoke, then all of a sudden her lips moved. I leaned as close as I could to hear her and she whispered more clearly than anything she had spoken over the past few weeks, "I wish I were dead."

PART II

*"I don't want to be sent
away somewhere to die."*

5.

Why should I have been surprised?
Hunters walk the forest
without a sound.
The hunter, strapped to his rifle,
the fox on his feet of silk,
the serpent on his empire of muscles—
all move in a stillness,
hungry, careful, intent.
Just as the cancer
Entered the forest of my body,
without a sound.

—MARY OLIVER,
"The Fourth Sign of the Zodiac"

IT WOULD BE nice if Margaret had changed her opinion over the next twenty-four hours, but she did not. The life she was clinging to was not one she wanted. She, who had always been in control of things, was helpless. Her nurse, and the night nurse who replaced him at the end of his shift and who was equally caring, sponged her, monitored all the instruments that surrounded her, tried to get her to swallow a little water mixed with gelatin or a spoonful or two of Jell-O, administered her medications, antibiotics against infection, steroids to bring down swelling of the brain tissue, painkillers, a medication to prevent seizures, and much more, all injected into a port in one of her IV lines. They rubbed ice on her lips; they were never farther than a few feet away behind the glass wall of the nurse's cubbyhole outside the room.

Their total concentration and undivided attention were impressive. They were, to use a word that may seem old-fashioned in the high-tech and often impersonal world of modern health care, unfailingly *kind*. Margaret slept, or dozed, her eyes were closed or unfocused, she occasionally mumbled something, but the words were unclear. On the second day I felt her hand squeeze mine, and our eyes met. Wherever she had been—who knows where the mind wanders to after more than four hours of full anesthesia and brain surgery?—she was back.

Over the next couple of days she was able to sit up a little more, and to speak, although it was still a struggle for her to find the word she was looking for, and harder still to pronounce it. She wanted to know how the horses and cats were; she did not ask about her own condition. In any case, the most Dr. Alain and the other doctors would say was that she was progressing normally, or "as expected." I emailed a progress report to one of Margaret's friends that sums it up: "Margaret still struggling to speak or choose the word she wants . . . Still VERY uncomfortable, much pain, words still very unclear or simply wrong . . . dozens of wires, tubes, monitors, alarms, &c. and of course she is terrified and angered at her inability to communicate. Also beginning to realize that it's a long, hard road ahead, no overnight miracles. She has lost much, MUCH weight, the words I heard most clearly from her today were 'Belsen' and 'Dachau,' but she did eat most of a bowl of butternut squash soup tonight, her first food in four days . . . All her food is puréed of course, and she can't drink liquids, like water, they have to be mixed with gelatin to make a kind of slush . . ."

Margaret could not hold a knife, fork, or spoon, or even her own ChapStick. She could not lift a glass, it had to be held up so she could sip slurry through a straw. Her nurse, who was unfailingly cheerful and confident, made the first step toward progress on this front. He took the metal cutlery from the plastic tray home and brought it back the next morning twisted into strange shapes, so that the handle was set at a ninety-degree angle and carefully wrapped with several layers of surgical cotton pads held in place by surgical tape. With these Margaret could just bring a bit of food to her lips if it was puréed for her. It required constant supervision to prevent them from being taken away when the tray was removed, but over the next year we managed to hold on to them in the hospital, at rehabilitation centers, and at home, all a tribute to his expertise. Certainly there was nothing on the internet that was nearly as useful or better designed.

By the third day Margaret was a little more animated, although she was still tethered firmly to her bed by the various tubes in and out of her body and by the cables and leads that connected her to the monitors that recorded every heartbeat, breath, and variation in her temperature, their presence producing a constant low hum and occasional pinging. Clearly, she was going nowhere until these had been removed. Her speech had improved to the point where she was able to ask when she would be able to get her hair washed, which I took as a good sign. I talked to Dr. Alain about this on his rounds. His judgment was that the dressing on her head could come off on the fourth day, and if everything looked good, then one of the nurses could shampoo her hair the next day. Perhaps more important, her catheter could be removed. This was all good news for Margaret. Dr. Alain reminded us that about three weeks from surgery she would need to have Gamma Knife radiosurgery, a procedure about which we should have no concerns, despite its name. No knife was involved, it was simply a powerful, precisely focused dose of radiation to kill off any remaining cancer cells in the tumor bed, an outpatient treatment without serious side effects.

When did he think Margaret could go home? I asked him. He thought she could be discharged on the sixth day, although he was still strongly in favor of her going to a rehabilitation center before going home. I tried that on Margaret several times over the next few days, but she still shook her head vigorously at the suggestion. In the mornings, before I left for the hospital, I interviewed speech and physical therapists, trying to get everything lined up for Margaret's return. All of them seemed well qualified and helpful, but none of them was enthusiastic about the house. Was I planning to replace our bed with a hospital bed? Had I given any thought to how she would get in and out of the bath? (Our house doesn't have any showers.) Some years ago, in anticipation of old age, I had asked our friend and neighbor Sam Reichelt to put a handhold at every place where he thought I might need one. Sam was an artist with wood, a man who stocked his own guns, and at my suggestion he looked up the handholds on the big ocean liners of the thirties, and reproduced them so perfectly that they looked as if they had always been there. It was the kind of big project he loved. He installed a separate bannister against the wall so I would be able to grip with both hands going up or down the stairs, and put checkered stainless steel handholds in the bathrooms as well. Here, at least, was one area in which I was reasonably well prepared, but the general feeling was that I had seriously underestimated the difficulties the house would present to Margaret. Nobody liked the polished eighteenth century wide-plank flooring that is one of the house's more appealing features, still less the rough stone walkway to the front door, which would be hard to manage for someone using a walker.

When I arrived at the hospital one morning I was astonished to see the dressing on Margaret's head had been removed, her hair had been washed, and she had been freed from most of her tubes and wires—I felt a combined sense of relief and apprehension. She was beginning to look like herself again, but she did not seem to me anywhere near physically ready to go home. Dr. Alain had been as good as his word, he had only cut a neat strip of Margaret's hair from below her left ear to the top of her scalp, but even without the white gauze turban that had covered her head fully, she still had a layer of white bandages.

Nobody's first steps with a walker after serious surgery are easy—Margaret just managed to shuffle her way up and down the corridor of the Neuro-ICU trailing her IV pole behind her, with her nurse and me at her elbows. There were, of course, no steps, no stairs, and no wooden floors there to trip her, but she returned to bed exhausted. I personally thought a few days more in the hospital would be good for her, but in the absence of any medical necessity Medicare and the hospital discharge the patient from the Neuro-ICU after a fixed number of days, this is simply not negotiable, so I busied myself finding an ambulance to take Margaret home on the day of her discharge.

But when the day finally came and I arrived at WMC, Dr. Alain met me and took me to one side. "Margaret has agreed to go into rehabilitation before going home," he said. I was astonished, and asked how he had persuaded her. He shook his head; it was her own decision, she apparently came to the conclusion herself that she wasn't ready, so I quickly signed the paperwork and the ambulance I had hired to take Margaret home took her to the Burke Rehabilitation Hospital in White Plains instead before she changed her mind. Margaret was always a realist when it came to what she could and could not do, she had always known exactly how far she could push herself and her horse. She was not one of those combined-training riders who are so eager to move up a level in competition that they end up with a lame horse or a broken neck. She could not be forced into doing something she didn't want to do, but she could be guided toward it gently until she made up her own mind. Clearly Dr. Alain had done that.

∽⁓⊃

Margaret's arrival at Burke was not a happy one, she would later compare it to entering hell. The move from the hushed ambience of the Neuro-ICU where she had her own nurse to a busy, crowded rehabilitation hospital dismayed her. I could keep telling her until I ran out of breath that she was going to do fine here, but I could see she was miserable—all the more so since there wasn't a private room for her. There was a zippered curtain between her and the other patient, who talked nonstop on her cell phone at the top of her voice, and whose large, noisy family filled the other half of the room, playing video games, watching television at high volume, and shouting at each other.

I could see that at any moment Margaret was going to demand to be taken home, so I pushed the curtain back and asked as politely as I could for them to quiet down a bit, explaining that Margaret had just had brain surgery. That made no difference, it simply raised the voice level, and produced an instant wave of hostility. I went off in search of a nurse, but she said she couldn't do anything about it. The nursing supervisor, when I found her, said she had more important things to do, there were no private rooms available anyway, so I went downstairs to find someone in authority. I couldn't find anybody in charge, and nobody in the admissions office seemed to know what to do, but by chance I managed to collar a doctor, who said it wasn't his job. "Well, *make* it your job," I shouted.

Concern for Margaret had managed to turn me into what I least like to be, an angry, combustible, unreasonable pain in the ass. With a sigh, he followed me to the elevator and we went upstairs. The people on the other side of the curtain were making as much noise as ever, but he ignored that, called for a nurse, and began to take Margaret's blood pressure instead.

It had been a long day that seemed to have gone on forever, although there were a least four hours to go before visiting hours were over. It had been less than three weeks since Margaret's diagnosis. All the tension, fear, anger, and concern simply boiled to the surface and I heard myself screaming like a madman. Later, after the explosion, I was reminded of Lear's words: "I shall do such things—What they are yet I know not, but they shall be the terrors of the earth." Impotent rage. I cursed, I threatened, I promised lawsuits, I would take Margaret home at once . . . The entire floor fell silent, while I raged on, temples throbbing, drenched in sweat. I should not have been surprised; although he never turned it on me, my father was known to have had a temper that could bring a soundstage to a halt and leave people quaking.

I paused for breath, and the doctor made a quick call. Within a few minutes Margaret was in a quiet private room, not quite as nice, or with as good a view, but *hers*. She squeezed my hand gratefully, and from then on I was treated by the entire staff as if I were a hand grenade with the pin pulled.

Now that Margaret had a room of her own, I was able to bring her clothes from home the next day, hang them in a closet and store them in the drawers, and put her things in the bathroom. I took it as a good sign that her sense of color and choice of what clothing she wanted returned to her. She was specific about exactly which shirts, bras, panties, trousers, and jackets she wanted, as well as exactly which handkerchiefs and socks I was to bring. She liked colors to harmonize rather than to match. Often, in the past, when I came downstairs dressed to go out to dinner she would send me back to choose a different pocket square or tie. One of the things she liked about Dr. Alain was that his clothes always harmonized, he too obviously had a discriminating taste for colors. Her second husband Burt had more neckties and pocket squares than any other man I've known, bought over the years at Turnbull & Asser in London, from Sulka in New York, or from Hermès in Paris, and could spend a long, thoughtful time picking out the right combination while Margaret paused from finishing her makeup to give him her advice. When they separated after a long and acrimonious divorce, Margaret carefully cut the tail off all Burt's neckties with a pair of pinking shears before leaving the apartment.

⁓◡

It cannot be said that Margaret grew to *like* Burke. It was big, busy, and noisy, visiting hours seemed to go on until late at night with no apparent restriction on the number of visitors, and there was of course not the intimate, one-on-one connection that had existed between patient and nurse in the Neuro-ICU. On the other hand, she had a vigorous daily schedule of physical, speech, and occupational therapy that kept her occupied, and kept me busy pushing her wheelchair back and forth from one session to the next. At the end of every session there was a crush of wheel-chairs at the elevators, which took considerable time to sort out, and Margaret was as determined to maneuver her wheelchair to the front of the crowd as she had been to win a horse competition.

Not unexpectedly, she was superb at physical therapy, her balance and her strength in the gym astonished the therapists, but speech therapy went slowly, and so did occupational therapy. Remembering words and pronouncing them was a challenge that almost reduced her to tears. I was deeply impressed by the speech therapists—I felt, as I would come to feel about so many people over the next year, awed and humbled by their devotion and the degree to which they were determined for Margaret to succeed. Still, her progress was slow.

I had not given much thought to occupational therapy, but it turned out to be much more difficult than I had imagined. Margaret quickly mastered putting square pegs in square holes and round pegs in round holes, but she still found it difficult to use a knife, fork, or spoon, or to take the cap off a pill bottle. The connection between her mind and her hands was still tenuous and unreliable, and she still seemed to have very little control over the fingers of her right hand. Writing was a slow, difficult process, something she had to learn all over again, like going back to first grade. Margaret's occupational therapist was sympathetic and briskly practical. Since our house has stairs, she made Margaret put her walker to one side and go up and down the fire stairs over and over again, with one hand on the railing.

Burke seemed to have thought of everything, there was a model kitchen off the gym so the patient could practice household skills and tasks, there was even a refrigerator with milk cartons, and more important a neat model bathroom where I could practice getting Margaret in and out of the empty bathtub, and she could practice getting on and off a toilet. The bathtub was the most difficult challenge of all. Getting her *into* it was hard enough, but getting her *out* of it was much more so—and she was dressed in gym pants, a hoodie, and sneakers; it would be a very different story when she was wet with soapy water and the Johnson's baby oil she always poured into her bath! We experimented with a number of different solutions, the most promising of which was a "medical adjustable bathtub shower seat chair with removable back," which had rubber anti-slip tips on the legs, although that meant that Margaret would not be able to lie back in the water. She would in effect be sitting in the tub to have a sponge bath. The most far-fetched device was an electric bath lift, which would lower and raise her out of the tub, but it proved more of a hazard than a help. A mat to prevent her from slipping would obviously be necessary; I made a mental note to add one to the list of things I needed to buy. Combining all this with a handheld shower that attached to the faucet by means of a rubber hose looked like the best way solve the bath problem without totally rebuilding the bathroom, which we didn't have time for. Anyway, the whole process of a bath seemed precarious to me, and I wasn't confident in my ability to lift Margaret out of the bath or to prevent her from slipping. No matter how many times we practiced this, it still felt risky.

Margaret characteristically downplayed the risk. She understood that Burke was something like the convent she had hated so much as a child, where she wasn't allowed to go home for the weekend until the nuns gave her passing marks for her classes and her behavior during the week and the Mother Superior had approved. Here, she would not be discharged until she had made enough progress in all her therapies to satisfy the medical director, and that was all the incentive she needed. It did not make her like the medical director any more than she had liked Mother Superior. She had an ingrained distrust since her convent days of all authority figures. Thus, when it came time to have the sutures removed from her scalp she did not trust anybody at Burke to do it, so Dr. Alain volunteered to come down to White Plains with a pair of surgical scissors and tweezers in sterile bags and take them out himself, which he did with his usual precision. There are surely not many neurosurgeons who would take the time to leave their office and perform what amounts to a physician assistant's job in a hospital not his own, but he had an understandable pride in his own skill, and a real interest in his patient—had he not become a neurosurgeon he would have made a good psychoanalyst. Margaret always felt that he was on her side whatever the circumstances, and also assumed that whatever the problem might be, he would take responsibility and would solve it, not a viewpoint that necessarily endeared her to nurses, PAs, other doctors, or hospital administrators, since it undermined their authority. Dr. Alain's patience was remarkable; he did not mind, or did not object, to being drawn into disputes about whether or not she could wear her own clothes to the gym or how soon she would be able to go to her hairdresser in New York City.

He perhaps understood as well as I did that these concerns masked the reality—she preferred not to ask the questions that *really* worried her. Would she be able to walk, talk, ride, drive, and eat normally again? Was she ever going to be the person she had been? What were the chances of the tumor recurring? Was she "cured," or was this merely a reprieve?

Shortly after Dr. Alain removed Margaret's sutures, I asked him about a call I had received from a friend in the city suggesting that there were new targeted therapies for melanoma, and wondering whether this was something Margaret should pursue. Dr. Alain replied that what I was referring to was immunotherapies for melanoma, and that it would be a good idea to get an appointment with Dr. Harriet Kluger at Yale, who was the expert in that field, and in fact he had already discussed her case with Dr. Kluger. I floated this idea to Margaret, but she had no interest, she shook her head angrily, it was hard enough to get her to focus on the Gamma Knife radiation, the scheduling of which was a source of disagreement between Dr. Alain and the medical director at Burke. There was no love lost between Margaret and the medical director, she regarded Dr. Alain as being in charge of her case, top of the chain of command, although he had no particular authority at Burke. Dr. Alain wanted her to have the Gamma Knife radiation as soon as possible, the medical director did not think she was ready to leave Burke, but a compromise between them was eventually reached. Speech was still difficult for Margaret, but she managed to express herself forcefully about the medical team that had to decide when she was ready to be discharged as if it were "the Politburo," as she put it.

In the afternoons, after the therapy sessions were over, I pushed Margaret around the grounds in her wheelchair, an outing we both enjoyed. At some point in the past, perhaps when Burke had been a private house, somebody had gone to a good deal of trouble and expense to create an Italianate cloister enclosing a formal garden. It was a pleasant enough place, with trees, bushes, flowers, lots of birds; not exactly a beauty spot, but at least it was outdoors, and even on rainy days it was possible to go around and around the cloister, breathing in the open air without getting wet. Margaret saved the little plastic packages of oyster crackers that accompanied her soup and I crushed them up to feed the birds. She had never been an indoor person. Even at home she was not good about being cooped up, as she put it, in bad weather, and chafed at the short winter days when the sun in our part of the world set by four o'clock in the afternoon. It was not just a psychological problem, it actually affected her physically, the way certain plants open up in daylight and close at night. Being wheeled through the garden—it was almost always deserted, apparently all the other patients were watching television or chatting with visitors—did her almost as much good as the physical therapy, but she dreaded the long nights alone in a strange place.

"I'm never going to come back here," she said to me one afternoon. "If I get sick again, or if I don't get better, I want you to just let me go." I told her she was going to get better, it was just a question of time, that she was making good progress, but she squeezed my hand hard and said, "I *mean* it."

The general opinion had been that Margaret would need at least ten days of rehabilitation before she was ready to go home, but by the end of a week she had made enough progress that there was no reason to keep her longer. She could make her way using her walker, she could go up and down stairs, she still had a long way to go when it came to speech and the use of her right hand, but thanks to Colleen I had already ascertained that she could get outpatient speech and occupational therapy at MidHudson Regional Hospital in Poughkeepsie, only a quarter of an hour's drive from home, and continue her physical therapy there as well.

~⸎⸎⸎⸎⸎ ⸎

She was more than ready to go, indeed she chafed at every delay, at all the paperwork, and she was terrified that the medical team at Burke might at the last minute find some reason to keep her there, but eventually it was all done and a nurse pushed her wheelchair out the front door to the waiting car. I had been assured by Dr. Alain that Margaret no longer needed to be transported by ambulance, so Rob Tyson helped her out of the chair and into the front seat of her own car. Her gym clothes hung loosely on her— she had lost nearly twenty-five pounds, and had been thin to begin with; when she managed to get on the scale at home she weighed 103 pounds. She closed her eyes and gave a sigh of relief. Thanks to Medicare, she had been given a parting gift of a walker, and a cane for when she could give up the walker. I stowed them in the trunk and we left for home.

She sat stiffly, her bandages hidden by a baseball cap that she had asked me to bring from home embroidered with "Kent School Horse Trials," where she had competed and won so often over the years. "I always had good luck there," she said when she put it on, and perhaps she hoped it would bring her good luck now. I had thought she would go straight to the barn when she got home to look at her horses, but once we had unfolded her walker she made straight for the front door, slowed by the fact that the wheels bumped and snagged on the uneven stones just as I had been warned. There was one big step up from the porch, which required lifting the walker up, then another from the dining room to the hall—no house could have been more poorly designed for an invalid. She paused there for a moment, a look of determination on her face, then she pushed the walker over to the foot of the stairs, grabbed both banisters, and slowly climbed up on her own step by step while I came up behind her in case she fell backward. I knew exactly how many steps up there were, I had counted them, thirteen, not an auspicious number. Given the age of the house, the steps were not as even as the ones in the fire stairs at Burke, and the staircase here was narrower and steeper as well. Nevertheless, she kept going, pausing for a moment once she had both feet firmly planted on each step.

When you think about it for a moment, we go up stairs by placing one foot on the next step as we climb—it is an automatic, sequenced movement—but Margaret could only go up one individual step at a time, so each was a separate challenge. By the time she was upstairs I was sweating myself as I counted to thirteen, from anxiety rather than from physical effort. I had bought a second walker to keep at the top of the stairs, so she was able to move herself from the banisters into the bedroom, where I helped her sit down on the bed.

"A triumph," I said.

"It doesn't seem like much of a triumph to go upstairs to my own bedroom," she replied, but in fact it was—a small one, perhaps, but a necessary first accomplishment. I wondered if she would ever be able to go up and down the stairs on her own, but put it out of my mind. The fact that she *was* home was already a big step forward, the first part of the healing process. I understood why she had not gone to the barn when we arrived, much as she must have wanted to see her horses—she would tackle one challenge at a time, at her own pace.

"We'll get you downstairs for tea," I said.

"Yes, perhaps."

"And tomorrow out to the barn."

She nodded. I untied her sneakers and took them off, then she got her legs up on the bed and leaned back on the pillows—*her* pillows. She took her hat off and handed it to me. "For God's sake, don't put it on the bed," she warned—it is an old English superstition: a hat on the bed brings death into the house.

Until I met Margaret I had been tossing my hat onto the bed for years without giving it a second thought. For somebody who was irreligious, she cherished a wealth of rural English superstitions: magpies brought bad luck like a black cat crossing your path, a peacock feather in the house brought death, spilling salt or opening an umbrella indoors were both bad luck, as was seeing a priest or a nun walking alone. My years in the Royal Air Force had inured me to superstition; most air crew are deeply superstitious, devoted to a lucky charm or to the belief that it is good luck to piss on the tail wheel, or the nose wheel of a more modern aircraft, before taking off, and horse people are just as superstitious. I suppose doing anything in which you risk your life or your neck tends to make you superstitious. At any rate I never flew in the RAF without making sure I had my lucky coin, a gold sovereign given to me by my Aunt Alexa, stowed in a zippered pocket of my flying suit. Now I carefully put Margaret's hat on top of the chest of drawers in the dressing room. I respect other people's superstitions even when I do not share or understand them.

I went downstairs to bring up Margaret's bag, and when I came back both the housecats were lying beside her: Ruby, the gentle one, curled up against her legs, the more aggressive Kit Kat purring noisily at her feet. They looked like sisters, though they were not. Considering that Ruby had spent most of the time while Margaret was away hiding in the linen closet, and that Kit Kat seldom ventured upstairs, regarding the ground floor as her own domain, this current arrangement was unusual: they would not normally have been lying on the bed together. I do not like to anthropomorphize, so I don't pretend to know what the cats thought, if they thought anything, but a degree of empathy, perhaps even sympathy, was unmistakable here. They knew Margaret needed comfort—and a welcome home—and they supplied it. Clearly, they had missed her as much as she had missed them.

The trip home and the climb upstairs had exhausted Margaret emotionally and physically, and she slept for a while, which was fine with the cats, it was pretty much what they wanted her to do—cats are big believers in an afternoon nap. I woke her at tea time, pulled on and tied her sneakers, then we made the trip downstairs for the first time. It was slow work. Going down was more challenging than going up, I had to go down backward step by step in front of her, since otherwise I would be unable to catch her if she fell. Going down a flight of stairs backward felt odd, in fact seemed like just the kind of thing a person my age *shouldn't* be doing. We always used to joke about my doing foolhardy things that might send me to the emergency room, like taking a fence that was too high for me while we were out riding, and that somebody in the ER when I was brought in on a gurney would say, *Silly old fart, what was he doing on a horse at his age anyway?* Or going downstairs backward with my hands outstretched to catch Margaret if she fell, I thought.

It seemed like a recipe for disaster. Still, Margaret made it to the bottom, grasped her downstairs walker, took the one treacherous step to the dining room thanks to Sam Reichelt's deftly placed handholds, and on into the kitchen, where she made a pot of tea despite her trembling hands. Getting a milk carton out of the refrigerator was harder than anticipated despite all the occupational therapy, but Margaret at last succeeded in making a cup of tea without a tea bag, and with real milk instead of one of those little plastic containers of creamer. We're English, we don't have the equivalent of the Japanese tea ceremony, so there's nothing sacred about the making of tea. But from her childhood Margaret knew that the teapot needs to be warmed first with boiling water, as well as exactly how many caddy spoons of PG Tips she needed to put in it (including the vital "one for the pot"), how long the tea had to steep after it was stirred, and to pour milk in last. Tea is as near to a ritual as English daily life produces. She held her mug up to her face with both hands and breathed deeply, while I unwrapped a straw for her and put it into the mug. She took a sip and gave a sigh of relief. She was home at last.

One by one over the next few days Margaret took her first steps back toward the life she had left two weeks ago. She had a bath after tea, which turned out to be just as difficult as predicted, in fact even worse. It took nearly an hour, left us both exhausted, and made me begin to question my respect for Margaret's strong feeling that she didn't need or want a nurse living in the house. As it turned out, our bathtub was lower than the one at Burke and therefore easier for Margaret to get into; on the other hand, just as I had expected, it was hard to get her *out* of the tub. Also it had a more rounded rim, and so it was precarious when Margaret sat on it to dry herself. The bathtub chair was not a success since using it meant that Margaret was essentially sitting *above* the water rather than in it, but on the other hand the non-slip mat—it had little suction cups to keep it in place—worked well enough. I could see that clearly Margaret's bath was going to be one of the more difficult moments of the day for both of us. It was not just the bath itself; Margaret's fingers were still unresponsive, so she was unable to manage buttons, bra hooks, or zippers. My attempts to do these things were slowed down by poor eyesight and stiff, clumsy fingers—I had reached the stage at which I had already given up on the tiny buttons of my button-down shirt collars, as well as cuff links and collar stays. When it comes to looking after somebody, willingness will only get you so far; certain basic skills are required, and I wasn't sure I still possessed them. Her illness would certainly bring us closer together, although in ways neither of us could have foreseen.

Margaret didn't eat much of the chicken quesadilla I had brought in from a nearby Mexican restaurant she liked. Nothing tastes quite the same after it has been chopped up into tiny pieces—in no time at all the quesadilla turns into unappetizing lukewarm mush. But she sipped a bit of her first vodka tonic with half a lemon squeezed into it since her surgery, and waited patiently while I assembled her prescriptions for the night against a carefully prepared checklist—it took a dinner plate to hold all the bottles of her medications—and went to sleep in her own bed at last.

The next morning demonstrated what I had already begun to perceive as a basic fact about home health care. Everything takes at least twice as long as you had supposed it would. Getting Margaret's teeth brushed and dressing her for the day took an hour before she was ready to make the trip downstairs, plus time for pills and breakfast, so she didn't make her first trip to the barn until the regular morning coffee break in the tack room, which takes place after the horses have been ridden and somebody has driven down to the Dunkin' Donuts in Pleasant Valley.

Margaret bumped her walker along the stone pathway, across the driveway, and up the one big step into the tack room, which was, in a very special way, her space, as much a reflection of herself as my office is to me. On one wall above a bench with a generous pillow were the plaques of her national victories, and on the others were photographs of her favorite horses, some retired, some dead, along with two neat rows of bridle hooks and saddle racks. There was a big, sturdy rack for cleaning saddles, an overhead hook for cleaning bridles and reins, a glass-fronted medicine cabinet, and two old-fashioned tack trunks. Some tack rooms are so expensively decorated that they look like extensions of the house, but Margaret's had evolved over the years from primitive beginnings into a place that was at once cozy and functional—everything was where she wanted it, from her boots and spurs to the big chest on which she kept her daily planner and wrote down which horse was to go into which paddock, and the time it went out and came in. Everything metal—buckles, bits, and spurs—was gleaming, everything leather was carefully cleaned with saddle soap or oiled with Lexol, there was a kind of solid, old-fashioned comfort in the sight of so many things that were honorably well used, worn by her knees or her boots, and perfectly looked-after for years or decades. Some tack rooms look as if they had been designed by a fashionable decorator, others are such a complete mess that you might hesitate to sit down. Margaret's was neither. It was home to the barn cat Tiz Whiz and a nice, unpretentious place for a dog to cool down or warm up depending on the season. Miguel, the barn manager, had brought her usual morning coffee, a small French vanilla with one cream and one Sweet'n Low, and had already put the straw in it for her. She sat for a while on the bench and brushed Tiz Whiz, as soothing for Margaret as it was for the cat, then she got up and wheeled her walker into the aisle in the barn to visit her horses.

Miguel cut up an apple for her from the barrel in the feed room and she gave a piece to each horse. They recognized her instantly. Horses don't have the possessive qualities of a cat or the soulful gaze of a loyal dog—you visit *them*, they don't visit you—but you could tell by the way they whickered softly and held out their nose to be patted that they knew her, even Logan go Bragh, her big black event horse, who is inclined to be standoffish.

She stood there for a while, breathing in the stable smells, and said, "I wonder if I will ever ride them again."

6.

"THE THING YOU have to understand about Margaret," I once told a friend of ours, Dr. Avodah Offit, a New York City psychoanalyst, "is that despite appearances she always remained a country girl at heart." When her marriage to "Gorgeous Don" broke up in 1960, she moved from Nyeri to Nairobi, where she met her second husband Burt, who was in Kenya photographing a travel story for one of the big magazines, and returned to the UK with him, and from there to the U.S. in 1961. She and Burt married as soon as her divorce from Don was decreed final, by then she was living in the big apartment on Fifty-Seventh Street and First Avenue near Sutton Place that Burt shared with his friend Clay Felker, founder of *New York* magazine and visionary godfather of "New Journalism," who did much to launch the careers of Jimmy Breslin, Tom Wolfe, Gloria Steinem, Gail Sheehy, and Gay Talese. Although Clay would marry the movie star Pamela Tiffin in 1962, the atmosphere of the luxuriously furnished apartment, with its baronial fireplace and a dining table that could seat fourteen, remained somewhere between that of a rowdy frat house and the newsroom of a big-city newspaper. Both Burt and Clay were cigar smokers who tended to leave their clothes scattered around the apartment, as well as newspapers, magazines, and photographs.

They were both dressy men who spent a fortune at the best tailors in London and New York, but neither was neat—Clay often looked as if he had slept in his clothes, Burt was apt to toss his beautifully tailored jacket carelessly on the nearest chair. They loved good company, the more of it the better, and liked to eat out every night at whatever the "in" media restaurants of the time were—in fact, Clay once boasted to Tom Wolfe that he had only eaten dinner at home eight times the past year, he had gone to the trouble of looking it up—and neither had any apparent interest in, or gift for, domesticity. How Margaret managed to survive this baptism of fire in the red-hot center of New York's journalistic elite during what would later be looked back on as the "Swinging Sixties" is hard to imagine, let alone how she managed to get Burt out of that apartment into one on Central Park West overlooking the park, but she transformed herself overnight into a glamorous clotheshorse—with closets full of haute couture—who traveled all over the world as Burt's model.

This was as far from country living as you could get, unless you counted a weekend in the Hamptons as country life, which she did not. Meeting "the right people" and making the right connections was Burt's concern, none of hers. Even so, the model— and the perfect hostess that she almost instantly became—must have been buried somewhere in the horsewoman and colonial adventurer, to appear so quickly. It was as if fashion sense and arranging sumptuous black-tie dinner parties full of celebrities had been bred into her, waiting to emerge, although that can hardly be the case, since Margaret grew up in the solid, unpretentious comfort of the farm manager's house in Overbury, Worcestershire, near the village of Broadway, which has since become a tourist destination, but was then a pleasant country backwater. She had a remarkable ability for becoming what other people wanted her to be while remaining herself at the core. It was not a process, or something she studied, and certainly Burt was no

Pygmalion; Margaret simply seemed to know how to take wing and fly effortlessly from one incarnation to the next. Beneath all that, however, she remained the girl who had started to ride at the age of three and was given her first pony at the age of four. Among her most treasured possessions was a photograph of herself on Snowy at about that age. At some point in the early 1970s she took up riding again, in Central Park in the mornings, and gave up accompanying Burt on his travels to every corner of the globe as his model for *Holiday, Travel & Leisure, Ladies' Home Journal*, and ad campaigns for Foster Grant sunglasses, Canadian Club whiskey, airlines, and cruise ships. That was when I met her, trotting around the reservoir in Central Park.

Although she may not have realized it—certainly Burt did not—she was looking for a return to her roots, to country living and horses. It was not surprising that she conflated recovery and riding; I did not think it would be long before she got back on one of her horses, even if she had to approach the mounting block with a cane.

But first came the Gamma Knife radiation, which took place at Northern Westchester Hospital's Cancer Treatment and Wellness Center, where we had first met Dr. Alain. These were more congenial surroundings than a huge hospital like Westchester Medical Center. Over the next few months we grew to like the nurses and to feel as much at home as you can in a place where you didn't want to be. Behind the comfortable waiting room with its cookies, pillows, tropical fish, verdant greenery, music, and soothing colors, the real work of cancer treatment went on in a businesslike way.

We arrived early in the morning, Margaret dressed as instructed in loose, light clothing. She was not wearing any jewelry, just her wedding ring and her watch, which I put in my pocket. She was fitted with a metal frame secured to her head with sharp pins, scary to look at, but not painful, a topical anesthetic prevented her from feeling anything more than a sharp prick, and she was given an intravenous sedative. Shortly afterward she was wheeled away for a preoperative MRI to determine the exact position of the target. In less than half an hour she was back, while Dr. Alain and his radiologist Dr. Julie Choi drew up a customized treatment plan, perhaps the most crucial part of the procedure, since it involved focusing multiple beams of radiation on one precise spot in the brain. While we waited, the data from the scan was transferred to a computer in order to establish "the optimal isodose plan and configuration" aimed at "the tumor resection bed in the left frontal region of the brain," where the surgery had been performed three weeks ago.

Although we did not yet know it, the scan also revealed two small metastases "localized to the contralateral hemisphere," in other words the *right* side of the brain. This dramatically changed the odds, since the appearance of two new tumors in the *opposite* side of the brain, small as they might be, was an indication that Margaret's troubles were not over, despite the successful resection of the large tumor. It seemed to me like a long wait before Margaret was taken to the treatment area, and the discovery of the two small metastases perhaps explains it. The treatment plan was more complex than anticipated, since there were now three separate targets instead of one. Fortunately, Margaret was sufficiently sedated that she didn't notice the length of time.

Behind the big doors marked with a radioactivity warning sign, Margaret "underwent the gamma knife stereotactic radiosurgical intervention in an uneventful fashion," to quote from Dr. Alain's postoperative report. Some people panic when the big, hemispherical metal collimator that directs each pinpoint beam of radiation from over two hundred different angles to focus precisely on the tumor is put in place, others when they are fed headfirst into the cylindrical opening in the machine. For anyone who suffers from claustrophobia this must be a terrifying experience, but Margaret didn't have a problem with confined spaces, nor wide-open ones either. She had no phobias except for a country girl's slight dislike of swimming in the ocean, perhaps natural to somebody born in Canterbury, Kent, and brought up in the Cotswolds—the sea seemed to her an alien place, not like the gentle rolling hills of rural England. She didn't mind pools, but always said that the most difficult part of her modeling career was the amount of time she had to spend on beaches and cruise ships for Burt's photo shoots pretending that she was enjoying it for his camera.

When the doors opened and Margaret was brought out, she didn't seem any the worse for wear. In fact, she was quite cheerful. Here, at least, was a major medical procedure that didn't involve pain or rehabilitation, hardly worse, in her words, than going to the dentist, except for the overwhelming size of the equipment. The frame was removed from her head, the small pin sites were treated with Bacitracin ointment and her head was wrapped in a full dressing, following which we were both served a light breakfast, quite a good one, in fact. The Northern Westchester Hospital's Cancer Treatment and Wellness Center goes out of its way in every detail to make the patient feel comfortable and at ease, it might serve as a model for cancer centers in many much larger hospitals. Everybody involved was friendly, cheerful, and positive, as if "wellness" were their chief business rather than "cancer." Whoever thought of naming the place "Cancer Treatment and Wellness Center" had a stroke of genius—there was no hint here of the icy remoteness with which cancer patients are often treated by the staff in many other places, perhaps a natural adaptation by the staff to having to know—and give—so much bad news during the course of every day.

This is not a phenomenon limited to the United States. In his brilliant book *Do No Harm*, about "Life, Death, and Brain Surgery," the English neurosurgeon Henry Marsh describes many instances of emotional distancing from the patient, not only among the overworked staff of nurses, physician assistants, and hospital administrators, but among the surgeons, including himself. (Marsh balanced this out by subsequently writing another book, *Admissions*, that includes his own experience as a patient.) To the cancer patient, particularly one who is going to be coming back again and again to the same place, the small niceties make a huge difference—there is probably no other time in life when the "human touch," so often lacking, makes such a difference.

Dr. Alain appeared, dapper and affable as ever, to assure us that the radiation had gone well, Margaret need not have any concerns, it had eliminated any cells remaining in the tumor bed and, he added, taken care of two small metastases, which should give her no further problems. Margaret did not seem concerned about the two small metastases, nor, I have to confess, was I. It sounded like "tidying up," and I felt grateful they had been found and eliminated. In hindsight I should have been more alarmed, or more curious. No fault attaches to Dr. Alain for this. Faced with a serious medical problem, patients (and those who are close to them) tend to hear what they want to hear, and what Margaret and I both wanted to hear was that the surgery and the radiation had been a success, she could get on with her rehabilitation and her life.

I do not think it had fully penetrated to either of us as yet that the key word about her brain tumor was *metastatic*, as opposed to *primary*. A primary brain tumor develops in the brain and remains there; a metastatic brain tumor has traveled to the brain from elsewhere in the body. When Margaret had a melanoma removed from her cheek five years earlier, either the surgeon had not "got it all," as surgeons are fond of announcing, or more likely Margaret had waited too long before having the spot on her cheek examined by a dermatologist. Either way, the cancer had already begun to metastasize—possibly in the form of the small asymptomatic nodules the radiologist noticed on both Margaret's lungs—and cells from these places eventually traveled through the bloodstream, crossed the blood-brain barrier, and flourished in her brain, in much the same way that cells from metastasized prostate cancer tend to travel to the spine and the pelvis. Every cancer seeks its own hospitable spot to develop and grow, and most cancers have a default position in the human anatomy toward which they move once they metastasize. As early as 1840 a British surgeon, Samuel Cooper, had traced the course of a metastatic melanoma and noted that "the only chance for a cure depends upon the early removal of the disease," and his prognosis has not significantly improved since then. Margaret's "disease" had not been removed early enough.

To understand why, it is necessary to take a small step backward. In 2007 my hairdresser, Paul Kelley, asked me if a dermatologist had ever looked at the "stuff" on the top of my scalp. What "stuff?" I asked. I had never felt anything there when I combed or brushed my hair, and since it is impossible to look at the top of one's own head, I had never noticed anything. Paul said he was no expert, but if he were in my shoes he'd have it checked out by a dermatologist. Although I am whatever the reverse of a hypochondriac is, I made an appointment to see a friend and neighbor of ours, Dr. Vincent Beltrani Jr., a dermatologist. I was not worried, but after all, I told myself, Paul spent his day looking at the top of his clients' heads, and he was no fool. If he saw something, then perhaps something was there.

As it turned out, what Paul saw there while he was cutting

my hair was a large malignant melanoma, for which I had surgery and a skin graft at Memorial Sloan Kettering in New York City. This proved to be an altogether bigger deal than I had anticipated, and once it was all over and the skin graft had healed I was left with a wide, shallow crater about three inches in diameter in my scalp, with a raised rim of scar tissue around it. I did not mind, I wore a hat as often as possible, and so long as I had enough hair I could brush it over the site of the surgery easily enough. Margaret was brave about it, as she had been about my prostate cancer years before, but I remember the look in her eyes when Vinnie Beltrani Jr. called late at night with the results of the biopsy—it was, briefly, one of terror.

More important, she inevitably saw the result of the excision and the skin graft every day—at first it looked like a badly healed war wound—and it would not be difficult for her to imagine how something like that would look on her cheek, with the result that when she *did* notice an irregular brown patch on her right cheek she put it firmly out of her mind, and dealt with it by covering it up with Clinique Superbalanced makeup; a light touch, and it was gone. With fair skin and a long history of sun exposure, or as we would soon learn to call it, sun *damage*, Margaret had plenty of freckles and sun spots, what was one more, after all? She was not one to stick her head in the sand like an ostrich in danger, but at the same time she wasn't an alarmist, and certainly not the kind of person who would run off to see a doctor every time she noticed a small change in her skin. Perhaps she also unconsciously associated a melanoma with what had been done to my scalp, and didn't want anything like that done to her cheek. In any case, when I finally noticed the spot and suggested that she see Dr. Beltrani, she didn't want to go, and kept putting it off—by that time she may have suspected that she might be getting news she didn't want to hear.

Eventually, I succeeded by a ruse de guerre. I asked Vinnie Jr., a keen car collector and motorcyclist, if he would mind stopping by unannounced the next Sunday to show me his latest car, and perhaps take the opportunity for a discreet look at the spot on Margaret's right cheek. He agreed, and no sooner was he out of his vintage TVR and into the house than he glanced at her cheek over a glass of water and said, "Why don't you come to my office tomorrow so I can take a closer look at that." It was not a question, it was a command.

Margaret had known Vinnie Jr. for years. She liked and trusted him—his father, also a distinguished dermatologist, lived down the road from us—and there was no way she would ignore Vinnie, so the next day we saw him. He immediately identified the spot as a lentigo maligna melanoma, and persuaded her to let him take a sample of it for biopsy. Vinnie Jr.'s notes describe the spot. "On the right cheek, there is an extremely prominent, irregularly-pigmented, ill-defined, 2 x 3 cm brown patch [which] she has been covering with makeup for many years." He performed "a narrow 1.6 x .02 cm incision . . . through the central portion of the lesion."

Once that was done, and the wound was closed with three sutures, he sat Margaret down and discussed in great detail the meaning of his diagnosis, a serious heart-to-hearter. Faced with the reality—Vinnie did not have any doubt that the biopsy would confirm his diagnosis—she was shaken but calm, and heard him out. He carefully explained that "the biopsy will clarify if the lesion is in situ or there is an invasive component"—that is, how deeply it had penetrated from the surface of the skin, the epidermis, toward the subcutaneous tissue where the blood vessels and lymph vessels lie. (An in situ melanoma is on the surface of the skin; its opposite is described as "in transit," which is to say there is a possibility of its traveling, that is, metastasis.) He discussed the possibilities of treatment with Aldara cream as opposed to surgery, making it clear that if the pathology report "reveals an invasive component, surgical solutions would be more appropriate." He was an early enthusiast for Aldara, but he mentioned it this time with an uncharacteristic note of caution. Vinnie was a friend, his manner was gentle, caring, sympathetic, he was careful not to elevate Margaret's level of anxiety, but he left her in no doubt that the melanoma was dangerous and that she would have to take it seriously. Delay, he made it clear, would not be a good idea.

Three days later the dermapathology report confirmed Vinnie's diagnosis. The results effectively ruled out treatment with Aldara cream; Margaret needed surgery, and the sooner, the better. The report succinctly summed up the bad news. "Sections show markedly sun-damaged skin with confluent growth of atypical melanocytes along the dermal-epidermal junction and extending above it into the granular cell layer . . ."

This was the moment at which our lives became dominated by the melanoma. We had a sense of urgency, but no panic. For two weeks we busied ourselves with doctor-shopping, that most exhausting of activities, looking for a dermatological surgeon with whom Margaret would feel at ease, and if possible one who would excise the tumor and perform the cosmetic repair at the same time, rather than two separate surgeries. Naturally, almost everybody we knew turned out to have his or her own favorite skin surgeon, and also to have strong opinions about the choice between Mohs surgery, in which the patient waits while tissue is removed and examined one microscopically thin layer at a time until pathology indicates that no further cancer cells remain, or the more traumatic excision of the melanoma with adequate margins. But in the end we found a doctor with whom Margaret felt comfortable, and had the surgery performed on October 27, 2011.

We congratulated ourselves on moving fast, but with hind-sight it was not fast enough.

Or perhaps it had already been too late?

⁓⊃

Five years later, Margaret experienced no side effects from the Gamma Knife radiation except for extreme fatigue—despite the fact that she applied herself to her rehabilitation with her usual determination. Thanks to Colleen Sinon, we managed to get Margaret's physical, occupational, and speech therapy in sequence on the same days so we would not have to spend the whole day going back and forth. MidHudson had recently been expanded, reno-vated, and redecorated. Its rehabilitation therapy was contained in a new atrium, another striking, modern piece of architecture—everywhere one sees the signs that hospitals are being run like competitive businesses, for better or worse. Only a few years ago the center of this hospital had been a crumbling Victorian build-ing; now it had become gleaming glass, with valet parking. The Physical Therapy Department is up-to-date and state-of-the-art, and Margaret had the great good fortune to meet, and almost immediately to bond with, Christopher Dayger, a slim, supremely fit, and engaging physical therapist who got her competitive juices going at once. Of course, Margaret was the ideal patient from a physical therapist's point of view—she had been extremely fit *before* her brain surgery, she loved physical challenges, and she liked Christopher and wanted to earn his praise. She actu-ally looked forward to physical therapy, particularly the balance machine, in which she did exercises on a rocking platform wear-ing a harness like that of a parachute in case she fell, while focus-ing her eyes on a moving target. Under Christopher's guidance she was able to exchange her walker for a cane in a couple of weeks, another big step forward. Speech therapy, predictably, went more slowly, but she did her homework after every session, despite the continuing difficulty of using her right hand. It would be difficult to imagine a place or people more determined to see her succeed, and Margaret's day became like that of an athlete in training. No sooner had she graduated to a cane than we took to walking every day, building up to almost three miles, half of it uphill. Somewhere deep in her mind Margaret equated fitness with survival.

About three weeks after coming home, Margaret took what was for her the biggest step of all. She came out as she did every morning to have a cup of coffee in the tack room and give Tiz Whiz, the barn cat, her morning brush, looked at my horse Montage, who had just been ridden and was still tacked up, and said, "I think I'll get on him."

Miguel and I exchanged glances. I nodded. Monty, a western paint, was far and away the most reliable and good-natured of our horses. Margaret had taken him from being a humble packhorse on a Montana dude ranch with brand on his shoulder to a combined training champion, and in all that time he had never given her a moment's trouble. No horse is ever *completely* safe, but Monty was as safe as they come.

Margaret made her way out through the barn and down the short ramp to the mounting block, Miguel helped her up the steps while I took her cane, she put her leg over Monty and sat down in the saddle with a sigh of pleasure. With Miguel holding Monty's bridle, she walked him twice around the big oval paddock without incident, then came back to the mounting block and dismounted.

She was smiling for the first time in more than five weeks.

7.

MARGARET STARTED TO take her life back bit by bit. Although her fingers were still clumsy, she was soon able to communicate with friends by email from her cell phone, short messages with many mistakes, but at least she no longer felt quite so cut off. She walked every day with her cane, increasing the distance day by day. I drove her to shop for fruit and vegetables at Adams Farm Market and to the supermarket, to MidHudson Hospital for her therapy and to Styling Sunsations to have her hair washed. She was tired, still reluctant to speak on the telephone, the right side of her face was still partly paralyzed, so eating was difficult enough to prevent her from going to a restaurant, but at least she was making progress.

On June 6, six weeks after Margaret's brain surgery, she emailed her friend Liz Benney: "I have only been able to email very recently, having lost the capability of doing so completely a few weeks prior to surgery. And even now I make so many mistakes, so keep them short. I don't have to tell you that I have been through a terrifying journey . . . A four and a half hr. brain surgery, a week in the ICU, followed by twelve days at Burke for rehab . . . I started in a wheelchair, then a walker and now a cane, which I often do not use . . . Everybody tells me that I have made terrific progress since getting home, I even got on the mounting block and sat on one of the horses last week! But will I ever ride out like I used to, I wonder . . ."

The next day she took an even more ambitious step, about which she emailed Megan: "I took a walk whilst Michael was riding, got on Monty when he got back and walked [him] once around the Oval, then drove my car to get my hair washed—with Michael with me, of course." Doctors and physical therapists had all been uncertain about when or even *if* Margaret could drive again, and were reluctant to be pinned down to a date for it, but in the end she decided for herself that she was ready and simply said, "Why don't I drive?" when we went to the car. She drove more carefully than she had in the weeks before her surgery, when she had seemed to me to be driving too fast and passing slower drivers a little too close for comfort. She was not nervous or over-cautious now, she simply took it slow, for a change.

None of this is to say that progress was easy, or linear. Every step forward exhausted Margaret. She who had always had enough energy for two people now found herself lying down for much of the afternoon. Everything, even the simplest task, took forever to do. She stabbed away at her cell phone to compose emails to old friends, spending what seemed like hours to send a message of only a few lines, or, worse, erasing it by mistake. "Tend to get a bit tired," she wrote to her goddaughter Tamzin Blinkhorn in the UK with typically English understatement, but then added: "This is a medical journey I would not wish on anybody." To Andrea Addison, the sister of her friend Robin, whose ashes we had sprinkled next to the stone wall in Margaret's "Field of Dreams," the eight-acre, perfectly cared-for field that contained her favorite jumps and which was kept as green and flat as a cricket pitch, "This morning I made it up The Field Of Dreams, and sat on the jump next to Robin, oh, how I wish he were here." That was her reward for the long uphill walk to reach the field—to sit for a few minutes on the stone wall she had jumped so many times and "chat with Robin," who had been dead for five years.

Margaret was sleeping badly despite the sleeping pills and all the exercise—getting up at night to go to the bathroom meant waking me so I could turn on the lights, come around to her side of the bed to help her out of it, give her her cane, then hold her arm as she made her way to the bathroom and back again. She seldom went back to sleep again afterward and was somewhat envious that I did. All the exercise in the world isn't enough to erase the anxiety that keeps you awake. The pursuit of physical fitness as defense against cancer is a delusion; of course exercise is good, regaining physical strength is important, but it's not necessarily going to stop the cancer from spreading. The enemy within doesn't care how many miles you've walked, or ridden, or biked, it has its own remorseless agenda. As my friend Julie Houston, a cancer victim, now dead, put it, "There is so little control . . . over cancer that one reaches out to anything—exercise, nutrition, what have you—as something to hold the illness at bay. These placebo activities provide something to *do*, rather than just sit back passively, at the mercy of the medical world."

Margaret was the person least likely to "sit back passively, at the mercy of the medical world," she pushed herself hard even as the temperature climbed, as if she were in training for something. Before her cancer diagnosis she had the gift of fitness without working for it, her horses kept her slim and fit—luckily for Margaret, what she loved doing most was also good for her—but now she had to work hard at it every day, and hated every moment of slogging on in the heat and the humidity, cane in one hand, fly whisk in the other. There is more to "walking the course" than you might suppose in combined training. The walking part of the course may be two or three miles long, before the cross-country phase, in which there must be careful decisions on the best approach to each fence, wall, or ditch, and counting off how many strides the horse has to make before taking a fence. Margaret was a good, brisk walker, but walking for its own sake had hitherto not been part of her life. She took to it doggedly, but without enthusiasm.

I had kept Margaret's friends up to date from the onset of her symptoms until her return home, but now she was in touch with them again herself. To her hairdresser, friend, and fellow cat lover Tom Della Corte in the city she emailed: "I have started walking on the trails every morning, a little bit more each day . . . I would like to come and see you [in New York City] pretty soon, I look like such a wreck. Months since I had high lights and a haircut. My surgeon says I can have color, but you would know best. I have hair growing in where shaved off for surgery—the scar is at least five and a half inches [long]. But my hair is breaking off badly, and thin. And oddly enough, straighter than I have ever known it."

Margaret hesitated to go down and see Tom, worried that her appearance might put off others in the salon. I emailed her concern to him: "She wonders whether people . . . would be shocked at the sight of the scar. I think most people would simply think there is a beautiful woman who has had a bad time of it, don't you, sympathy rather than shock?" Tom told her not to be silly, promised to give her as much privacy as possible, and managed to perform a small, welcome miracle with her hair. Even so, as Margaret emailed a friend, "I have slipped backwards somewhat . . . Too much time indoors, I have always been an outside person, very active, bottom line is I feel depressed."

It was not a coincidence that Margaret's next MRI was scheduled for July 21, three months after surgery—as we would soon discover, her spirits plummeted toward the end of every sixty-day period as she approached the next MRI. She longed for the day when the interval between MRIs could be raised to ninety days. In the trip down to Northern Westchester Hospital in Mount Kisco for the MRI she sat stiff, dry-eyed, and silent in the car, looking very much like Jacques-Louis David's sketch of Marie Antoinette in the tumbril on her way to be guillotined in the Place de la Révolution. At any rate, things went smoothly this time, "MRI was good, no sign of new cells," Margaret emailed Megan, the next MRI would be in September. "I had gone downhill during the weeks beforehand from depression as to what the outcome would be," she wrote to a friend. "My surgeon told us that had I not had the surgery when I did, I would have been dead within two weeks the tumor was so large."

The first neurosurgeon we saw in Poughkeepsie had warned us that she might be dead in a matter of weeks if we didn't let him do a biopsy. Alain, who called often to see how Margaret was doing, and whom we both regarded as a good friend, now put her survival at two weeks if she had not had the surgery, and that *did* make Margaret feel that she had dodged the bullet, but it did not cheer her up much. Her life was now clearly divided into two parts, before and after brain surgery, and she wondered if she would ever be "the person I was before." It was a question she asked a lot, of herself, of me, and I had no clear or honest answer to it.

I had been putting off having my pacemaker-defibrillator replaced until Margaret had her first MRI, and since this turned out to be a slightly bigger deal than anticipated, our positions were briefly reversed as Margaret worried about me, but I shortly resumed my role, the most difficult part of which was trying to find things that Margaret *could* eat, since chewing was still difficult, and— a bigger challenge—also *wanted* to eat. Breakfast was simple, a banana mashed up so it could be eaten with a spoon; lunch was easy at this time of year, a slice of mozzarella and a tomato, chopped up finely and drenched with olive oil; dinner was more of a challenge, since everything had to be chopped or mashed: crab cakes, macaroni and cheese, Japanese takeout—improbably, Pleasant Valley, a hamlet with nothing much in the way of food except a thriving McDonald's, a diner, and Pam's Bun 'N' Run, has a good Japanese restaurant—and when I could drive over to Millbrook (I didn't like to leave her alone too long), I'd return with an order of excellent *sole meunière* with *gratin dauphinois* potatoes and green beans from Margaret's favorite local restaurant, Les Baux. All these dinners had in common that they were easily puréed or chopped, but Margaret never ate much even when it was something she liked. Struggling to feed herself with the special spoon we had taken from WMC was dispiriting, and when I fed her it seemed like a defeat to her. Given all the medications she was taking, the doctors at Burke had warned her against alcohol, but, with the civilized common sense of a fellow Roséen Alain overruled them and said he saw no harm in her having a drink every night. Margaret was never a big drinker, but her nightly vodka tonic with half a lemon squeezed into it had been an almost sacred part of her routine for as long as I had known her. Even when she was away competing she always took along a miniature airline bottle of vodka, a bottle of Schweppes tonic water, and a lemon, in case she had to have dinner at a place without a bar. Now she sipped her drink through a straw gratefully, although she seldom finished it.

I had never given much thought to the notion of being a caregiver, nor imagined I would ever be one. I totally understood Margaret's reluctance to have someone living in the house to look after her—she had a strong sense of privacy, as do I—but I had underrated the challenges it involved. Margaret and I shared most household tasks, we even stripped and remade the bed together like a team every Sunday morning. Of course, there were things we did separately. Margaret knew better than to ask me to join her to look for new kitchen mats at Kmart—my boredom level for that kind of shopping was low—and I did not expect *her* to accompany me when I took one of the cars to be serviced. After all, we were not Siamese twins, but we were together more often than many couples, especially after I retired. Now she needed help to do even the simplest and most basic things like tying her shoe-laces, dealing with buttons, or pulling up the zipper of her jeans, and caregiving became a full-time job. I had vaguely assumed I could fit it in with other things, editing a manuscript, working on a book, but I soon realized that everything took twice as long when there was only one person to do it, and that there were a lot of things I didn't know how to do and would have to learn. Getting Margaret's hair put up and pinned so it wouldn't get wet when she had her bath was one of them. I seemed to have no gift for using Magic-Grip hairpins or hair clips, and my clumsiness irritated Margaret almost as much as her inability to do it herself. Getting her in and out of the bath every afternoon continued to be the most difficult part of my day, and the one that left us both feeling helpless. She could no longer hold a razor, so I shaved her legs when they needed it, which turned out to be harder than shaving my face in the morning because it was a new task for me. Keeping tabs of Margaret's medications was by comparison an easier, although time-consuming task. There were so many that they filled a dinner plate in the middle of the kitchen table, and since they needed to be taken at different intervals, my assistant Dawn and I drew up a chart in many different colors so I had a guide to what she had to take and when. It took a while for it to sink in for both of us that our life together was going to be radi-cally different from now on, that so many ordinary things in life that Margaret had always done alone she now needed help with.

There is a new kind of intimacy between couples when one of them takes on the role of caregiver. In a curious way it brought us closer together than we had been in many years, which is not to say that it was without its occasional flashes of stress, impatience, and even anger when a zipper got stuck or I dropped a hairpin for the umpteenth time. We all like to think that we will be up to the challenge when worse comes to worst, and that it will all happen naturally, but none of this is necessarily true. Margaret was sometimes incapacitated by her fear of becoming helpless and by her anger at the fact that her whole life had been turned upside down at the age of seventy-nine, and I was sometimes overwhelmed by my new responsibilities and the decisions that had to be made. Of course, so long as Margaret's MRIs remained clean, these decisions could be put off for a time, but waiting passively for bad news did not seem to me the sensible thing to do.

Margaret had been resistant to the idea of seeing an oncologist when Alain first brought up the subject. Given her feelings about doctors, it was remarkable that she had developed such faith in him—she saw him as *her* doctor, the one in charge of her case, she was willing to do anything he wanted her to do, she had accepted surgery, rehabilitation at Burke, Gamma Knife radiation, all without a protest—or at least without digging her heels in—but she emphatically did *not* want to consult at his suggestion with Dr. Kluger, the distinguished oncologist at Yale Cancer Center in New Haven who runs immunotherapy clinical trials on advanced melanoma patients. So far as Margaret was concerned, Alain was in charge of her case, the equivalent of her *chef d'équipe* in combined training. She did not want another doctor, besides which she was reluctant to commit to a long series of treatments with no end in sight. As Alain wrote to Dr. Adam, her internist, "Margaret has indicated very clearly to me that she does not wish to pursue systemic therapy for her stage IV melanoma and expresses great anxiety with regard to any additional therapy."

This was putting it mildly. Alain had called Dr. Kluger, and his office made several appointments with her, all of which I was obliged to cancel with considerable embarrassment at the last moment, since Margaret did not want to be driven all the way to New Haven to be placed in a program of testing experimental drugs with potentially alarming side effects. She had a horror of becoming a patient, still more of being a guinea pig in and out of emergency rooms, her life an endless succession of hospital visits, tests, and consultations as she pictured it, not without reason. What good was giving her more life if it wasn't a life she wanted? she asked.

I am not sure either of us realized the extent to which stage IV metastatic melanoma would remain life-threatening even if the removal of the brain tumor was successful. The cancer was there in her body, it had been quiescent for over four and a half years since the melanoma surgery on her face, during which time she had remained completely asymptomatic, but now it was on the move, the brain tumor merely the first and most immediately threatening sign of what was going on. We do not hear what we don't *want* to hear, and Margaret was determined not to hear this.

I thought she should go to New Haven and hear Dr. Kluger out; she could always say no, after all. In the meantime I read up on advanced treatment for metastatic melanoma until it was a blur. Almost everybody I called in the medical world, and many outside it, had a list of medications Margaret should be on—had she tried Yervoy, had she heard about Opdivo, had her doctor mentioned BRAF inhibitors?—and stories about people who had been saved when they were at death's door, but Margaret was particularly resistant to hearing about any of this. As for me, I soon realized that you can read about checkpoint inhibitors, ipilimumab, or targeted therapy all you like on the internet, but that's not going to turn you into an oncologist, and for each medication the thing that first catches the layman's eye is the list of dire side effects. Picking one at random, it would have been hard to persuade Margaret to take something that might cause among other things "lung inflammation (causing difficulty breathing), rash or inflammation of the skin, hepatitis, inflammation of the kidneys causing decreased kidney function, colitis (causing diarrhea or bleeding), and inflammation of the endocrine organs (pituitary, thyroid or adrenal) . . ." any more than she would have wanted to have "salvage surgery" explained to her (it is pretty much what it sounds like). She dismissed the horror stories, of which there were many. What she wanted was to get back to something that resembled her life as soon as possible, for as long as that might be. She had painstakingly created that life for herself, the house, the barn, the horses, and she would cling to it for as long as she could rather than spending it in a hospital gown undergoing treatment in New Haven or elsewhere.

In that she resembled her father, Paul Mogford, who, when he had been moved into a "cottage hospital" (the English equivalent of assisted living) with emphysema and heart problems after a lifetime of chain smoking, simply turned his back on the treatment options and willed himself to die. Stubbornness was built into the Mogfords, along with a certain pitiless realism, and Margaret was in that way too her father's daughter. When her marriage to Burt was breaking up, she wrote a short story about her own suicide as seen through the eyes of her friend Mayo, who would actually commit suicide herself a few years later. "Silhouetted now, hair spread out, so all I could see was this wonderful mane and slim body . . . she sighed and from the position of her arms I could see that she had stuck her thumbs in her belt. As long as I had known her she had done this, pulling the belt and waistband of her jeans away from her body . . . 'You know,' she said, 'it's not the people any more that I think about, not even my mother and father. I always worried about how it would affect them. Now I don't. And I used to think, well there's that new movie opening next week, or we are going to Bali, or somewhere, and I would forget about it all . . . Not now, not any more.' "

I could talk to her about Dr. Kluger until I was blue in the face. Once Margaret decided she wasn't going to travel down that path, her mind was made up. She was always like that, a Scorpio, she had the courage of her convictions; once she had decided to make a break with something or someone it was immediate, permanent, and without regrets. Once she had decided to do something, it was done, set in stone, that was the spirit that had carried her to victory so many times, and brought her to the life she wanted. She did not waste time on second thoughts. Her good friend and fellow competitor Carol Kozlowski emailed Margaret shortly after her successful MRI. "I hear that you've fought bravely and are gaining ground . . . I guess I wouldn't expect any less from you. I'm hoping you'll find joy sitting on a horse again, even if you never step onto the competition arena again. I still have an image of you on Nebraska, fairly unbeatable, in my memory. So many wonderful memories, you've always been beautiful on horseback."

Beautiful on horseback was exactly what Margaret wanted to remain. She wasn't about to settle for a long, slow slide into the toxic side effects of immunotherapy and a life spent in ERs and hospitals. She was determined to re-create her life as it had been for as long as she could hold on to it. "Always good to sleep in your own bed," she emailed Carol Kozlowski when Carol told her she was driving home by herself from the Millbrook Horse Trials after competing with her horses to Geneseo, New York, a distance of over three hundred miles, instead of spending the night—exactly what Margaret would have done, was *doing*.

She was home, and determined to stay there.

8.

THE LIBRARY—or, as we called it more realistically, the "TV room"—of our house must have been built during a brief period of prosperity on the part of the owners back in the mid–nineteenth century, when there were still people around locally who knew how to do such things. It has nicely carved wooden shelves and cupboard doors, and a very pretty fireplace—nobody could call it "elegant," but it was at once handsome and cozy, unlike the larger, chilly living room, which we seldom entered. Margaret and I tended to gravitate to the TV room for a drink before dinner and a look at the news, and we often ate dinner there on folding TV tables and watched a movie or a miniseries, sprawled out on the big sofa with one or two of the cats beside us. Normally we would have gone out to dinner to celebrate our thirty-eighth wedding anniversary on June 30, but Margaret was still sensitive about the droop in the right side of her lips, so we stayed home quietly and celebrated in the TV room. By coincidence we had both written the same message on the card attached to each other's gift: "38! May we have many more!"

Since Margaret could only drink through a straw, I had bought her an antique Tiffany sterling silver bamboo-pattern straw, which would save me from bringing a fistful of straws back from Dunkin' Donuts every few days, and she had bought me a half bottle of champagne. We talked about taking a midwinter vacation, which we hadn't done for years, but without conviction. We did not talk about the disease, or the MRIs, or the side effects of the medications, which was perhaps our best gift to each other over the past six months—cancer so easily becomes the only subject of conversation, the unwanted guest at every celebration.

As the summer wore on, Margaret's strength returned. She was still too thin, the facial muscles on the right side of her face were still stiff, simple things like brushing her teeth were lengthy, infuriating tasks, but she was driving by herself now for short trips without me riding shotgun. Perhaps more important she graduated from riding Monty, the reliable old paint I had inherited from her once his competition days were over, to riding Logan go Bragh, her big black event horse—Logan was strong, "forward moving," as horsemen like to say, with a mind of his own, and plenty of power under the hood. He was too much horse for me—I wouldn't have ridden him on a bet—but it was interesting to see that when Margaret was mounted on him, she looked as if she had never been ill at all. She still needed a cane to walk, and needed help to eat or brush her teeth, but once she handed the cane to Miguel and mounted Logan she and the horse came together as one, it was a fine thing to see. It gave her more confidence too, and made the ordeal of waiting for her next MRI on September 22 a little easier to bear.

She described the two weeks leading up to the MRI as "tense and worrisome," but that is putting it mildly. It was not just that each MRI had the potential of being a death sentence, pronounced by a radiologist instead of a judge—each one put at risk all the effort Margaret had made to recover, the hours in the gym balancing on a narrow beam, or trudging up and down improvised steps and around obstacles, further hours of speech therapy and occupational therapy, and all the walking back and forth over our fields, despite the heat, the humidity, and the bugs. It was a huge investment of time and hope, all of which could be swept away in a second by the appearance of new tumors or the return of the old one. You could see the small signs of tension, the constant, nervous shredding of a piece of Kleenex into tiny pieces—was Margaret even aware she was doing it?—the time she spent out in the barn with her horses, listening to their quiet snorts, which are a sign of pleasure in a horse, stroking each silken nose, communing with them, the way she would stop while we were out walking and stare at the fields and fences as if she were trying to imprint all of it on her mind. It did not seem to her fair that all of this could be torn away from her, and of course it wasn't, disease never is. She had never believed in a God who punishes, she preferred not to believe in Him at all rather than that. She didn't believe either in the kind of moral equivalency that people express when they say consolingly, "Well, think of all the *good* years you've had . . ." as if the good years had to be paid for by so many bad ones, or that a formula existed by which so much joy and pleasure had to be paid for by an equal amount of pain. Sometimes Margaret asked why this had happened to her, but it was a rhetorical question. She didn't expect an answer, or even suppose there was one.

By now the secretary behind the desk in the Radiology Department welcomed us back as if we were familiar clients at a good restaurant. I held on to Margaret's hand until her name was called and waited patiently for her return. It was not a long process, there was never any significant waiting time, and when it was done we walked around the corner to the Cancer Treatment and Wellness Center next door to see Alain. Within a few minutes he appeared, smiling, to take us into his office and tell us that the MRI was clean. We were back out to the car in fifteen minutes,

Margaret looking years younger. "Dr. Alain very pleased with brain scan, huge sigh of relief," I emailed a friend.

The next MRI would be just before Thanksgiving.

It was a turning point. Starting the next day, Margaret began riding two horses a day again, just as she had for years before her illness. Her appetite improved. She still tired quickly, but at times she seemed like her own self again, although that was an illusion of course: cancer and brain surgery change the person in so many ways, nobody is or can be "the same" afterward. Whatever else she was, Margaret was no longer invulnerable. She had survived what seemed like the worst that could happen, but she had not emerged unscathed—nobody does. Her hair was growing back to hide the scar on her head completely, but she had a sense of the impermanency and fragility of things. She began to write cryptic random quotes in huge, uneven capitals in the small notebook she kept on her bedtable beside a photograph of her father and a red leather case containing the Royal Mint gold coin commemorating the coronation of King George VI in 1937, the year she was born: "Walking debris," surely an ironic self-description; "Yesterday's gone," perhaps remembering Brenda Lee's song, but perhaps also a wistful reference to her own life; "I have a rendezvous with Death," the first line of Alan Seeger's famous First World War poem; "Would you cross the Rubicon for me?" perhaps a question aimed at me? More mysteriously, "Remember the Ark was built by amateurs, the *Titanic* by professionals," and just below it, "Uncork time!" Of course she would want to go back to the time before the diagnosis of a brain tumor was made, which is perhaps why she added "Age of Innocence," a reference to the time when she could still ask, "What's the worst thing that can happen to me?" instead of living with the fact that it already had.

The days grew shorter as autumn began, the mornings began to be crisp, the leaves started to turn, it was sometimes even chilly—perfect riding weather, probably the best time of year in the Hudson Valley, "good sleeping weather" as they used to call it up here from the days before air-conditioning, when people put on a sweater and started to think about pumpkin pie and turkey. Margaret put on a little weight, not much, but she was moving in the right direction. Her hairdresser Tom had somehow managed to perform a small series of miracles to make her hair look good. I emailed a friend that things were beginning to look better.

I should have knocked on wood when I wrote that, or whispered, *Inshallah*, God willing.

Never tempt fate.

~~~

We celebrated my eighty-third birthday on October 8 quietly at home, it wasn't a "significant" one like seventy or eighty, we used it to celebrate the rate at which Margaret was recovering, clinking our glasses together on the sofa in the TV room. It seemed like old times.

But it wasn't. A week later her symptoms began to return with a vengeance, the trembling right hand, the facial paralysis, the problems with speech and finding the right word. They were minor at first, one could pass them off as fatigue, or perhaps the result of trying to do too much too soon, but a few days later it was apparent that we were back in full crisis mode. After a call to Alain her MRI was moved forward urgently, and with it the anxiety returned.

This time there was a lengthy wait between the MRI and Alain's appearance to show us into his office. We sat glumly next to the tropical fish tank in the slightly surreal surroundings of the Cancer Treatment and Wellness Center waiting room. The tropical fish did not cheer her up—she disliked the whole idea of confining any living creature in a cage or a tank, even fish, and for that reason she always avoided zoos. She was not a vegetarian— quite the contrary, she was happy to eat a Dover sole properly cooked and served—but she hated the idea of keeping anything trapped behind wires, bars, or glass.

"I know it's going to be bad news," Margaret said. "He's never kept us waiting before." The same thought had occurred to me, but I tried to reassure her: there might be a snag or a problem with the MRI, or Alain might have a patient with an emergency. From where we were sitting we could see the door to his office, and after some time we observed Dr. Julie Choi, the radiologist, go in and shut the door behind her.

"That's a bad sign too," Margaret said. "He never needed her help to look at my MRI before." Margaret had not, as they say, "bonded" with Dr. Choi during the Gamma Knife radiation, although I myself had found her perfectly pleasant, but for whatever reason the two did not seem to have hit it off, and the long time that Dr. Choi spent with Alain increased Margaret's anxiety sharply.

After a time Dr. Choi left his office, and Alain came out to greet us, with rather less ebullience than usual. The results of the MRI were ambiguous, he explained once we were seated. There were signs of swelling, perhaps a delayed reaction to the Gamma Knife radiation. His notes describe what he observed from his physical examination of Margaret, and from the MRI. There was, he wrote, "a slight increase in the right-sided facial droop . . . [and] decreased coordination affecting the right hand," as well as the fact that she "was taking smaller steps," which I had not noticed at all. I ought to be paying closer attention, I told myself. On the MRI he saw "a significant increase in the edema surrounding the resected lesion as well as a slight, but noticeable, increase in the size of the lesion," and "a slight increase in size of the much smaller right parietal lesion that was treated at the same time [that is, the time of the Gamma Knife radiation]." It was possible that "the increased size of the lesions could be due to the delayed effect from the radiation treatment"; however, it could also be a recurrence of the tumors, or worse still a combination of the two.

We sat in silence for a few moments contemplating all this. As was usually the case when confronting bad news, Margaret was stony-faced. Alain explained that a course of steroids might bring down the swelling, and prescribed dexamethasone, accompanied by Pepcid in case the steroids gave her stomach problems. I was to keep in touch with him about her neurological symptoms, and we should return for the pre-Thanksgiving MRI that had already been scheduled. Hardly any doctor could have been more sympathetic in giving a patient bad news than Alain; on the other hand, he did not hide the fact that Margaret's recovery was no longer a sure thing, if it ever had been. She had been making progress. Now she had hit a setback.

In the car on the way home she sat in front next to Rob Tyson, with whom she usually enjoyed chatting, silent and staring at the road ahead. Rob knew the signs of bad news and was silent too.

When we were home, Margaret put the kettle on and we sat down in the kitchen waiting for it to boil. "If I die will you look after my horses and cats?" she asked.

I told her I would, of course, but said it hadn't come to that. She should wait to see how she did on the steroids.

The kettle whistled, Margaret got up to make tea. She had never looked healthier or better since her diagnosis in April, she always made an effort in any case to look her best for Alain. She put a biscuit on the saucer of my cup for me. She shook her head.

"I can tell," she said, "I'm entering a new phase."

9.

THE "NEW PHASE" began at once, with a dizzying change of pace. It was as if the disease had been moving slowly until then, and now, after this latest MRI, everything was suddenly speeded up like fast-forwarding a movie; there was scarcely time to take a breath between one crisis and the next. It had been just over four weeks since the last MRI, which revealed the swelling in her brain, and the next one, weeks in which we waited to see if the steroids were working (they did not help), during which Margaret slipped back into anxiety and depression, and among other things ceased to be able to answer emails or grasp a knife, fork, or spoon—the fingers of her right hand were almost useless again. She wrote her last email, to Megan on October 20, as the leaves were turning and the nights were growing cold. ("I am hoping that the medications I am on start kicking in! To get the swelling down.") After that she had to dictate her replies to me to send from her iPhone, there was no way her fingers could do it. All her emails after that date began with my writing, "I'm replying for Margaret." Her speech regressed rapidly too, and not surprisingly her anxiety soared. Alarmed, I emailed Alain, "I think Margaret is going downhill very rapidly . . . loss of feeling in right arm below the elbow, and in right hand and right fingers, complete loss of appetite, huge apprehension (understandably)."

In the meantime, I read up on swelling in the brain—the correct medical term is "brain radiation necrosis"—on the internet, and soon discovered the Cancer Survivors Network of the American Cancer Society, which was chockablock with anguished and detailed entries from people who had experienced Margaret's symptoms or worse. These were not easy or comforting reading, one writer described herself as being not only sad but angry, other entries sounding more like rants, one ending that he did not like "this necrosis BS" and did not want to go through brain surgery again, echoing pretty much Margaret's feelings on the subject. Almost all the writers knew much more about treatment for brain cancer than I did. One wrote that her husband went through WBR [whole-brain radiation] and chemotherapy, then treatments of Taxol and carboplatin, followed up with Tarceva and one treatment of targeted radiation. I looked up the side effects of each medication and sighed. She added that she thought he would have been happier with a shorter life and being able to ride his Harley for a while longer. Obviously, I had a lot to learn about brain cancer, although as a motorcycle enthusiast from the age of seventeen I understood about the Harley. The general opinion was that brain radiation necrosis was almost as daunting as the brain tumors themselves, and could have a devastating effect. Another remarked simply, "Cancer stinks!" *Amen to that*, I thought.

The American Cancer Society's website is pretty much confined to the facts, and tends to put about as positive a gloss on things as you can on the subject of cancer and cancer treatment, but most of those who had experienced brain radiation necrosis, or their loved ones, were vocal naysayers who had apparently slipped through the review process and whose opinion was best summed up by that of Howard Beale, the crazed TV news anchor in *Network*: "I'm mad as hell and I'm not going to take it anymore."

I devoured as much as I could on the subject, keeping in mind that reading cancer sites on the internet was not going to turn me into an oncologist overnight—at best it might help me to ask more sensible questions after Margaret's next MRI. I did not think it would do Margaret any good to share with her the experiences of those who had brain radiation necrosis, there was simply no point in adding to her anxiety, and no reason to jump to the conclusion that the steroids would not solve the problem so long as there was still some chance they might. As for me, I struggled with alarm and despondency as I read about what lay in store for Margaret.

Everybody who lives with a cancer patient sooner or later has to confront the problem of how much to tell him or her, and, more difficult, how much the patient *wants* to know. Margaret, I knew from long experience, did not want to know the details, or read about what had happened to other people with the same problem. She wanted simple answers from Alain rather than long explanations from me. "What will happen to me next?" was basically what she wanted to know.

In the meantime, we faced Thanksgiving, of all holidays perhaps the most difficult to deal with for two people—it's hard enough to cook a turkey with all the trimmings for two people even if both of them are in good health, and nothing replaces the Norman Rockwell image of a large, abundant family gathering. Ours was bleak, and was made unexpectedly grimmer by the news that my former wife Casey had suffered a brain aneurysm on November 24 alone in her New York City apartment, and was not expected to regain consciousness. Her resentment over the breakup of our marriage had not cooled down a bit over several decades, and I regretted that we had never made peace. Too late now, of course. Of our closest friends, one was in hospital having a section of her bowel removed, another was in the hospital with pneumonia, a third had been hospitalized after a seizure and was now being treated for hydrocephaly. General de Gaulle, I reflected, was certainly right when he wrote, "Old age is a shipwreck."

As it turned out when the day finally arrived for Margaret's next MRI—postponed at the last moment when we were already there because the machine broke down, so we waited for a whole day beside the tropical fish for something that wasn't going to happen, feeling as trapped as they were—the subject of swelling in the brain hardly came up. I might have saved myself the time, trouble, and angst of reading up about it on the internet.

One always knows that when a doctor begins a sentence with "Unfortunately," something bad is coming, and that was indeed the case. Tactfully, gently, Alain broke the bad news to us. The MRI scan "shows further increase in the size of the two lesions such that we are now dealing with recurrent tumors as opposed to radiation necrosis," as he wrote the next day. In other words, both the original tumor that had been resected in April and the smaller ones that had been discovered before Gamma Knife radiation in May had returned and were growing rapidly. This was not just going back to square one, it was worse. There were now *two* tumors instead of one.

Alain was firm about what needed to be done—"surgical intervention" as soon as possible to "debulk" the two tumors, followed by a course of focal fractionated radiation. Would that mean entering the skull in two different places? I asked. Yes, he

said. Margaret was shaking her head, I saw that it was very doubtful she would agree to this. Would the process be the same? Going
somewhere for rehabilitation—I was sure Margaret would not go
back to Burke again—then physical therapy, speech therapy, and
so on, all over again? Alain said the process would be much the
same, and Burke wasn't the only place, of course. Margaret inter-
jected for the first time, what if she had the radiation *without* the
surgery? That would be better than doing nothing, he said, but it
was not what he would recommend; removing the tumors was the
first and most important step. What would the side effects of the
radiation be? There might be fatigue—he paused for a moment—
and significant hair loss.

I could see from the expression on Margaret's face that the
sooner I got her home, the better. The first brain surgery had
bought her less than seven months, she said quietly, most of them
miserable. How many months would all this bring her? That
was impossible to answer, Alain replied, a lot would depend on
her having a PET/CT scan of the chest, pelvis, and abdomen "to
determine the extent [of] her systemic disease."

This was something that Margaret had firmly ruled out. She
did not want to see an oncologist specialized in the treatment of
the melanomas, it was a can of worms she did not want to open—
if she was "riddled with cancer," as she put it, she didn't want to
know. We had too many friends who had gone down that road
and ended up in the hospital having treatments that were as bad
as the disease itself, suffering dreadful side effects without alter-
ing the outcome. I knew who was on her mind: Peter Forbath, a
swashbuckling *Time* foreign correspondent in the days when that
was still a glamorous profession, a friend of us both—nobody
had been more supportive when I was recovering from cancer
surgery—whose cancer diagnosis and treatment led to just the
kind of long and destructive illness that Margaret feared. I had
known others who went that route over the years, including the

Hungarian nuclear physicist Leo Szilard, to whom I brought the final page proofs for his corrections of *The Voice of the Dolphins* as he underwent cobalt therapy of his own devising for bladder cancer at Memorial Sloan Kettering Hospital, and Cornelius Ryan, author of *The Longest Day*, to whom I brought the proofs of *A Bridge Too Far* as he lay dying of metastatic prostate cancer. Both of them were robust and courageous, and it had been terrible to see them as their cancer—and the treatment—destroyed them day by day.

Margaret felt the same way, in fact even more strongly, about Peter Forbath's death—much as she trusted Alain, the likelihood of her going to New Haven to see Dr. Kluger was approaching zero. Later I would ask myself whether I should have pressed her harder to go, and Alain asked himself the same question, but the reality is that you cannot push people beyond the level of their comfort zone, and Margaret more than most people was resistant to being pushed. She was not suicidal, she did not want to die, she was prepared for a battle, but not for a long and losing siege of what is sometimes called, both by those who experience it and those who give it, "desperation oncology." Had she known what lay ahead in the next few months she might have chosen differently, but I doubt it.

"I can't go through a second brain surgery," Margaret said firmly once we were home. "And I don't want to go and see Dr. whatever-her-name-is."

"Harriet Kluger. Alain thinks you should."

"I know. But I remember what it was like at Sloan Kettering, I don't want to end up like that."

I sighed silently at the memory. At some point when I was doctor-shopping to decide where I would go and what treatment I would have for my prostate cancer, we got lost and walked through the radiation department looking for the doctor whose specialty was radioactive seed implementation, and who, like so

many specialists, once we finally found him, was a true believer—
surgery was no good, hormone therapy wasn't the answer, the
only sure thing was radiation, everything else was a total waste of
time. While searching for his office we walked down long corridors full of patients lying on gurneys or sitting slumped in wheel-
chairs, eyes vacant, tethered with wires and tubes to monitors and
IV bags and catheter bags, bald heads marked in various colors
to indicate the precise point of focus for the radiation they were
waiting for. It was a sight that was admittedly unsettling, like
opening a door and seeing something you were not meant to see,
but for Margaret it must have represented everything she feared:
helplessness, being treated like an object, misery. At the back of
her mind she feared that Dr. Kluger's immunotherapy program
would be something like that (a fear that as we were soon to
discover was not entirely groundless), she did not want to be "a
guinea pig," as she described it, in clinical trials of new cancer
treatments.

"You think I'm wrong?" she asked.

"I think I might feel the same way you do about repeating the
brain surgery. I'm not sure I could go through that a second time
either. But if I were in your shoes, yes, I would go and at least *hear*
what Dr. Kluger had to say."

"But you're *not* in my shoes. I'll think about it *after* I've had
the radiation," she said. "I suspect that's going to be bad enough,
without going to New Haven as well. And I'm not going to put
myself through another brain surgery, much as I like Alain. I just
can't. You'll tell him?"

I called Alain the next day to let him know that Margaret
agreed to have the radiation, but couldn't go through a second
brain surgery, and also didn't want to see Dr. Kluger yet, although
she might do so after the radiation treatments were completed. He
did not seem surprised. He would speak to Dr. Choi and get the
plan for the radiation started as soon as possible.

Later that day I emailed Alain to thank him for "breaking this bad news as gently as possible today," and asked him what would happen if Margaret did nothing, and how long it would be before the symptoms become terminally threatening. He replied promptly, frankly and thoughtfully. "Breaking bad news is never easy, this despite the fact that I have had to do this periodically throughout my career as a neurosurgeon . . . To answer your question, if nothing is done Margaret will have but a few months left, how many is impossible to say. As the larger of the two tumors expands her speech will become more impaired as well as the coordination of her right hand. Eventually her balance will be affected to the point that independent walking will become impossible. The terminal phase occurs when patients slip into a coma and eventually stop breathing."

Well, I told myself, *now you know.*

Had there still been any question of whether or not Margaret would go to New Haven for immunotherapy, it was resolved once and for all by a front-page story in the *New York Times* on December 3 headlined "Immune System, Unleashed by Cancer Therapies, Can Attack Organs."

There was never any chance of hiding this from Margaret even had I wished to, because the *New York Times* was placed in the tack room every morning next to her coffee. She still glanced at the front page, so she could hardly miss the headline. Dr. Kluger was the central figure in the story, which, while it offered a certain degree of hope for the treatments she was testing, noted "a risk of side effects that were severe, requiring hospitalization or were life-threatening 54 percent of the time." Dr. Kluger admitted, "It's at least that high, at least." The story went on to describe in harrowing detail the side effects and "devastating results," prompting another immunologist to remark, "I'm not sure you can get rid of the side effects—it's really what you want." You had to poison the body to destroy the cancer, in short.

The *Times* story pretty much killed off any chance that Margaret might change her mind about going to see Dr. Kluger. To be fair, some of Dr. Kluger's patients had their life extended even with stage IV melanoma, but one of them "spent 24 days in hospital, where trouble mounted, first his pancreas failed, then his bowels inflamed and his kidneys became dysfunctional"; another went into "diabetic ketoacidosis . . . when her pancreas shut down." Dr. Kluger took this setback philosophically. "Her pancreas isn't coming back," she said briskly. "She has her life."

Alain sent me an email the next day to say that after reading the *Times* story any enthusiasm that Margaret might have for "an immunotherapy may disappear." I agreed: "I have to say that the article makes it very doubtful that Margaret would want to risk something that has a 50%+ chance of making her very much sicker than she already is. Margaret's overriding desire is to be left in peace for as long as possible. Despite the limitations that her symptoms produce, she still drives and rides, and looks after her animals, cats and horses. She wouldn't want to enter a program that meant that she was going to be 'a patient' for the rest of her life, or going back and forth to emergency rooms, or dealing with side-effects and diseases almost as bad as what she already has, and perhaps worse."

Alain's reply was a model of courtesy and good sense. "Of course I understand the dilemma Margaret is facing. In the end we all want to have a quality to our remaining days, given that each and every one of us will sooner or later face the inevitability of our own mortality. To spend those precious few months dealing with the complications of treatment is not appealing at all. I do not think that Gamma Knife radiosurgery is out of the question for the smaller of the two tumors, but for the larger one fractionated radiation therapy makes more sense, given the size of the tumor. My suggestion is that this be discussed with Dr. Choi when Margaret sees her."

"I want Tamzin to have all my jewelry," Margaret said out of the blue a few days after the *Times* story.

A couple of weeks ago I would have told her not to be silly, or that there was plenty of time left to think about that kind of thing, but I merely replied, "Of course." Margaret had never wanted to be a mother, and in the years when that had been possible she made sure it didn't happen. Her second husband Burt had always wanted children, and so did his family, who expected Margaret to have them. It had not been the only issue that undermined the marriage, but it was a major one. She had made her feelings on the subject clear to Burt before they married, so they cannot have come to him as a surprise, he may have supposed that Margaret would change her mind once they *were* married, but Margaret never changed her mind about the things that mattered to her, and this one mattered to her a lot. It was not so much that she disliked children, she simply did not want to have one herself.

That did not mean that Margaret was totally without maternal feelings. She felt for Megan, who had worked part-time in the barn and ridden Margaret's horses for twelve years, a motherly concern, and felt the same and more so about her goddaughter Tamzin Blinkhorn, who had lived with us on and off for over thirty years, long enough for Margaret to come to feel that Tamzin *was* her daughter, particularly since Tamzin is English and a good horsewoman in her own right. Tamzin went on to have a successful career in commercial real estate over here, and when she finally decided to return to the UK for good in 2002 it felt to Margaret like losing a daughter. Like any parent, she had muddled feelings, pleasure when Tamzin married and had a daughter of her own, alongside the feeling of being abandoned after Tamzin returned to her roots three thousand miles away. Tamzin's mother and Margaret had been close friends since the age of three, and there was perhaps some unconscious transatlantic rivalry between them for the possession of Tamzin, but if so the competition between them was very English—everybody involved was polite, soft-voiced, it all took place without any visible emotion, indeed without anybody admitting, or perhaps even realizing, that it was going on.

I was glad that Margaret had decided to leave her jewelry to Tamzin, not that jewelry had ever mattered that much to her. Except for her engagement ring, a present from me, none of what Margaret owned was particularly valuable. She loved turquoise, jade, lapis lazuli beads, and interesting silver pieces from Santa Fe or Taxco, preferring visual impact to value. Given a choice between a piece of jewelry or a new horse, she would unhesitatingly choose the horse. Still, all of it, even the costume jewelry, meant something to her, she knew where she had bought each piece and when, or who had given it to her. I asked if she wanted to *see* Tamzin, but she replied firmly, "Not yet."

Few things are harder than telling someone that they're dying, unless it's doing the dying oneself. Not many people are good at breaking the ultimate bad news. Most doctors don't like to, perhaps because it's admitting to failure—it's one thing to pronounce someone dead, quite another to tell them that it's about to happen. The only people who are good at it are hospice nurses—it's often part of their job because nobody in the family has faced up to it yet; and Roman Catholic priests—after all you don't get the last rites until you're dying, being anointed with the holy oil is a sure sign. Rehearsing what you're going to say to the person who is dying doesn't help much, at any rate it didn't help me. When the moment comes you have to find the right words, though in fact that part is easy. "You're dying" will probably do it.

When you tell someone they're dying is more of a problem. If you delay too long, until communication has ceased, it may be too late, and by that time unnecessary. On the other hand, telling someone too soon is cruel. "Where there's life, there's hope," is a platitude that goes back to the time of Cicero and further, but we still want to believe it even when it is no longer true. We hope for a miracle, we hope for a delay, at the very least we hope for a "good death," whatever that is. Margaret was not naïve, she knew from the bad news Alain had given us about the MRI on December 7—"Pearl Harbor day, of course," she had commented with trademark irony—that she was "terminal," but terminal is not the same thing as dying, terminal is a process, not an end. Very few of us can *imagine* our own death. You can imagine what kind of ceremony you want, or how you want to be dressed when you are the corpse in the coffin, or how grief-stricken your loved ones will be (or you *hope* they will be), but nobody can imagine what it will be like to die. Margaret understood that things were going badly for her, but at the same time she was getting on with her life. She was about to start the radiation treatment, she made an appointment to see her dentist in New York for a routine checkup and cleaning, she was still getting a manicure once a week, riding two horses a day, walking a mile or two depending on the weather, carrying on, for how long of course nobody could say. The only person I knew whom I could ask about it was Thom Schwartz, a nurse who lived up the road. He said, "You'll know when it's time."

The one thing worse than dying is *wanting* to die, reaching that point at which pain, or anxiety, or physical decline, or all three, become so terrible that death seems preferable. Would Margaret ever reach this point, I wondered, and what would I do if she did? Christopher, my son by my previous marriage, had been a teenage evangelist of euthanasia, and cofounder of the Church of Euthanasia, although its purpose was to preach saving the planet by eliminating human overpopulation rather than relieving end-of-life pain. The publicity surrounding this movement and the means by which Chris and his followers promoted it had given his mother Casey, myself, and Margaret a good deal of grief way back in the late 1990s, and soured me on the whole subject of euthanasia, however well-intentioned. Besides, euthanasia is illegal in New York State.

I began to read up on terminal illness, starting with Atul Gawande's *Being Mortal* and moving on to Sherwin B. Nuland's *How We Die*, guiltily removing the dust jackets so Margaret wouldn't notice what I was reading, as if they were pornography. Both these books were brilliant, bracing, and informative rather than depressing, although it did not escape my attention that Dr. Gawande had not found it easier to make his father, also a doctor, face what was happening to him than the rest of us would. Dr. Gawande was afraid of telling his father, his father was afraid of dying and did not want to suffer—pretty much what any of us would feel in the circumstances. Nor did the fact that they were both doctors alleviate the father's suffering in the end: the medical Juggernaut moved on mercilessly, prolonging Dr. Gawande's life well after he wanted it ended. I consoled myself with the thought that it would surely take a considerable amount of time before we reached that point, if we ever did. After all, Margaret was about to start radiation treatment, and following that there would surely be further treatments. There would be plenty of time to think about all this when Dr. Choi had completed her work, six sessions of radiation spread over two weeks.

Looking back on it, I realize that my mind was deeply divided. On the one hand, I was thinking about what we needed to do on a practical level if, or perhaps *when*, Margaret's illness got worse; on the other, I was assuming that somewhere along the way *something* would work, giving her more time—that the radiation *might* help despite Alain's caution, that Margaret *might* in the end go to see Dr. Kluger or someone like her . . .

That in fact she had only four more months to live, and that everything she feared most would happen to her, was not yet apparent to me.

10.

*Ways must be found to de-medicalize the final weeks
or days, to nurture the dying and those who love
them, and by this means to nurture ourselves.*

—SHERWIN B. NULAND,
How We Die

MARGARET LOVED EVERY bit of Christmas: sending Christmas cards, displaying the ones we received, putting up the tree, decking the horses' stalls with Christmas wreaths, it was the holiday she enjoyed most, but in 2016, as this memo of December 8 to me from my assistant Dawn demonstrates, the Christmas spirit was notable by its absence, replaced by her radiation treatment:

Tuesday, 12/13 imaging, sometime in the afternoon
Wednesday 12/14, first radiation session
Friday 12/16, radiation
Monday 12/19 radiation
Wednesday 12/21, radiation
Friday, 12/23, radiation
Each radiation session will be in the A. M.

The first session would not prove to be particularly stressful, it entailed making an exact mask of Margaret's face so as to position her head correctly for the radiation. I found the technology of it all interesting, even soothing, but cutting-edge technology was not high among Margaret's interests. I could not help thinking that molding the plastic mask was a process strangely similar to that of making the death mask in the eighteenth and nineteenth centuries, when it was the custom to call someone in immediately after anybody of wealth or importance had died to take a plaster cast of the face from which a bronze impression could later be made, but I sensibly kept this gruesome thought to myself.

At any rate, there would be nothing hard and difficult about the radiation itself except for the amount of time it took to drive down to Northern Westchester Hospital and back. Perhaps inevitably, both Margaret and I developed what were perhaps exaggerated hopes for the radiation; with cancer one grasps naturally at straws, every new treatment seems like a potential lifesaver until it isn't. The fact that some part of my mind was operating more rationally is borne out by my email from the hospital to Dan Scharff, who looks after our house, asking him "to set up an alarm in Margaret's bathroom, in reach of the tub, that would sound and/or flash in the kitchen and in my office." Clearly, I was anticipating some substantial further decline in Margaret's ability to look after herself—although even then I was being overoptimistic, because there would very soon be no possibility of leaving Margaret alone in the tub without my presence.

The first radiation session produced an unfortunate hiccup, since it was canceled at the last moment, which produced a moment of extreme anxiety for Margaret—given that she had placed such hope as she had in the radiation, only to have it postponed when we were already in the car and on the way. I swiftly communicated with Alain, who was as always patient and responsive. The treatment plan, he explained, had to be "modified extensively" because of Margaret's prior Gamma Knife radiation and the fact that she now had two lesions instead of one, and Dr. Choi would be ready to begin it tomorrow. Margaret simmered down, but it did nothing to improve her feelings about Dr. Choi. The next day also proved disappointing and stressful. We spent the entire day waiting beside the tropical fish in the Cancer Treatment and Wellness Center while technicians came and went trying to repair the radiation equipment, which had broken down, and we were finally sent home late in the day with the promise that it would be working again in time for the session on Friday. The decorations in the waiting room did not produce much in the way of Christmas spirit under the circumstances.

The next forty-eight hours were understandably testy—Margaret felt like a drowning person toward whom someone had offered a helping hand, only to draw it away at the last moment. One of our friends emailed to ask after Pablo, who had worked in the barn for twelve years and was going home to Mexico (not perhaps perfect timing on his part), causing Margaret to erupt in indignation and dictate a reply that I sent under my name. "[Her] first concern . . . is not that Pablo is leaving, but that [the] malignant, metastatic brain tumor has returned, in addition to another one appearing in a critical place in the brain, all extremely bad news," and adding on my own: "What she needs at this moment in her life is concern, love, caring and physical/emotional support . . . Hugs, care, love, tears should go to her, not to Pablo . . . What we need now is a miracle."

⁓

We did not get one. There is no handbook on how to communicate with someone suffering from a terminal illness. I came to realize that however close they may be, most friends don't find it easy to say or write the right thing. There is a balance between chitchat about one's own life intended to distract the patient and heavy-breathing concern that simply makes the patient even more depressed or anxious, hard as it is to strike it. As Margaret lost weight—she was already "thin as a stick," I wrote to a friend—she increasingly did not want visitors. She made an exception for one of her friends, a passionate cat lover and fellow horse person, who begged to see her, then sat down for tea and talked nonstop for one hour about *her* cats without once mentioning Margaret's illness. You could see in her eyes that she knew she was getting it wrong, but she was unable to stop—she could not bear to ask about Margaret's cancer, or the treatment, or Margaret's feelings and fears, in the end she gave her a quick hug and kiss and left in tears without having reached out to Margaret in any personal way. It would have been funny had it not been so sad. Margaret simply sighed, and said, "I don't want to go through *that* again." Nor did I. I thought to myself, how difficult can it be to ask Margaret how she feels, how she is dealing with it all, and whether there's *anything* you can do to help? And then perhaps talk a bit about good times they have shared?

The truth is that we don't want to ask about what we don't want to know. Terminal illness scares people, it's almost as if the patient were contagious. Particularly when somebody as physically strong and active as Margaret gets sick, *really* sick, people think, *If it could happen to her it could happen to me*, a thought nobody wants to cling to. Margaret might as well have hung the Sword of Damocles above her guest's head at tea.

～◯

The radiation session on Friday finally went smoothly enough, there was no drama and no immediate aftereffect, in fact the treatments all proceeded as planned on schedule. They made Margaret noticeably more tired and she was more often unable to remember things. We had been warned about that, and at the same time her ability to use the fingers of her right hand deteriorated further. This was enough to make me ask Colleen quietly, without spooking Margaret, whether we could find a good home-care service in the neighborhood that might be covered by Medicare.

As Christmas approached, Margaret started losing her hair— we had been warned of that too, but it was still a shock when it began to happen. It's one thing to think about it, and another when great tufts of hair fall into the sink every time you comb or brush it, or tufts cling to the pillow when you wake up in the morning.

For as long as I had known her, Margaret had always done Christmas on a grand scale, sending countless cards with long handwritten notes, supervising Christmas trees, wreaths, and decorations, getting everything "just so," even if it was only for the two of us. But now she could no longer write, or hang up cards, or arrange Christmas ornaments without breaking them, and her spirits plummeted. She did her best to carry on, but each present she tried to wrap was a challenge, and few of them came out the way she wanted them to. Alain halved her dose of steroids, which helped a bit, but it was a grim Christmas, waiting for the next MRI in the hope it would show that the growth of the tumors had been slowed, and we hardly even bothered to celebrate the new year. Wishing each other a Happy New Year felt false and uncomfortable, but we did it anyway, without conviction.

I spent the first week of 2017 talking to Margaret's hairdresser Tom about where the best place was to get a wig—I thought nothing would raise Margaret's spirits more than a good wig, and he recommended that we meet at Barry Hendrickson's Bitz-n-Pieces salon at Columbus Circle, giving me a whole new subject to read up on; I soon knew more about wigs than I had ever wanted to. In case Margaret wasn't up to going to the city Colleen pursued a separate search closer to home, but in the end a snood turned out to be the best temporary solution. Friends FedExed hoods, caps, and snoods of every description, even one woven out of bamboo fiber, but a simple plain black one seemed to work best. Very soon, however, the rapid decline in Margaret's condition unexpectedly eclipsed the question of what to do about her hair.

A more pressing concern to me was that Margaret had no doctor locally in case of a crisis. I worried about what we would do if something went seriously wrong over a weekend or at night—a seizure, for instance. Her internist Dr. Adam was in New York City; Alain was in Westchester, and in any case he was a neuro-surgeon, among the most specialized of specialists; Dr. Tom was an ob-gyn on the verge of retiring; and our neighbor Dr. Vinnie Jr. was a dermatologist. Who would we turn to in case of a sudden problem? Vinnie, at my request, had suggested an oncologist in his group, Dr. Jason Rubin, but Margaret did not want to see another doctor and was still deeply resistant to the idea of consulting an oncologist. I was concerned enough to send an email to Alain shortly after New Year: "Since [Margaret] completed the five sessions of radiation she has been exhausted (which Dr. Choi and yourself predicted), but she also has had a return of memory problems, speech problem, and difficulty with using her right hand. Is there any chance that these will diminish in time as the radiation wears off? I think she should also have an oncologist in Poughkeepsie, someone reasonably close at hand in case of further problems. Margaret does not want to do it, but it seems to me that it will be necessary at some point . . ."

Alain replied cautiously that there was no guarantee the radiation would lead to an improvement of Margaret's speech, memory, or finger problems, but he certainly thought it was a good idea for Margaret to have a local oncologist, even if she decided "to let things be and not pursue any more treatments." He added that it was normally the oncologist who coordinates the care of a patient with a cancer diagnosis, "including end-of-life care, as the latter can be the most difficult challenge both a patient and family face."

My eye was naturally caught by the phrase "end-of-life care," and I realized I had not been looking at the matter in the right perspective. If we were going to face the challenge of "end-of-life care," there were a lot of decisions that had to be made, and Margaret would have to be involved, however little she wanted to be. Mentally, we were still waiting to learn whether or not the radiation treatments had halted or slowed down the growth of the tumors, but Alain's message alerted me to the possibility that they might fail altogether, in which case Margaret would be caught in a downward spiral, there was no telling for how long. Dr. Choi had told us that Margaret's next MRI would be in six to eight weeks, somewhere between the beginning and the last week of February. In the meantime, we had an appointment to see Alain and Dr. Choi on January 12 to discuss the situation.

Margaret's symptoms were now worsening and multiplying at a rapid rate. She complained that her skin was becoming very delicate, "tears easily, heals very slowly," while her speech was increasingly garbled and her appetite dropped to zero. I reported all this to Alain, adding: "She talks of killing herself, and asks what she has to live for if she is not going to improve beyond this . . . I thought you should know all this before our consultation with you both on Thursday . . . Sorry to burden you with this, but I do not feel I can or should leave you unprepared. She is in a very bad way, frankly."

Alain replied the same day, reminding me ever so gently that he had recommended surgery before radiation, "as this would have had the advantage of reducing the volume of tissue [which] needed to be irradiated," and suggesting that Margaret have an MRI immediately before our consultation on January 12.

When I told Margaret this, she said quite calmly, "This is all going in the wrong direction, isn't it?" Perhaps because I was finishing *Alone,* my book about Dunkirk, I was reminded of the famous David Low cartoon in which a lifeboat is sinking with everybody at the stern, the little countries baling desperately, while John Bull and Uncle Sam sit at the bow and one says to the other, "Phew! That's a nasty leak. Thank goodness it's not at our end of the boat." I felt that we too were bailing as hard as we could as our boat went down, and that nothing could stop it from sinking. We had both expected a brief, if nervous, pause of six to eight weeks before the next MRI, perhaps followed if we're lucky by some relatively good news, but now the MRI was going to take place less than three weeks after Margaret's radiation treatment had ended, and it did not seem likely to produce any result that we wanted to hear.

"I should have had the surgery when he recommended it, shouldn't I?" Margaret was wistful, not angry. Except for the hair, she had never looked more beautiful.

"Yes, probably," I said. Choosing to have radiation instead of another round of brain surgery had been a mistake, that was already becoming clear. I felt, already, certain guilt at having let her make that choice, but I also understood her reluctance to go through the same ordeal again. On the other hand, just doing nothing seemed like giving up, and as Alain had made it clear the end was not likely to be easy or painless. Organs would break down, systems would collapse, death would probably take place in a hospital, surrounded by monitors, tubes, and wires. For the moment, Margaret was still riding, driving, grooming her cats, activities that soothed her nerves. So long as she could do all that, I thought she should continue to take whatever treatment was on offer to prolong her life.

That was probably a mistake, as well.

There was a certain consternation among the friendly, familiar faces at the radiation department of Northern Westchester Hospital when Margaret turned up for an MRI only three weeks after the previous one. Even the receptionist knew how to interpret that; there was no diminution of the cheerfulness which is de rigeur for people in the radiation department, but there was now a hint of sympathy and concern as well—an urgent MRI so soon after the last one could hardly be good news.

The consultation with Alain and Dr. Choi afterward went more quietly than I had anticipated. Dr. Choi sensibly kept a fairly low profile, and Alain, in his firm but tactful way, maintained control—in any event, the results of the "urgent MRI" were so awful that they prevented any outburst from Margaret about the aftereffects of the radiation, which had not only cost her her hair, but had no effect at all on the two tumors. Both of them had grown in size, in addition to which there were now three new smaller metastases in the brain. "The only reasonable option at present," Alain wrote to Dr. Adam on the same day, summarizing what he told us, "is the one I initially presented to her on December 1, 2016: namely, a surgical intervention to debulk both tumors." This would be preceded by another Gamma Knife stereotactic radiosurgical intervention to treat the three new metastases. "It is evident," Alain added, "that she will also need to have an oncologist for frank discussion with regard to systemic therapy, something which she has been avoiding all along."

Strangely enough—a tribute to Alain's persuasive power and tact—Margaret agreed to all this without argument. He made it clear to her that the alternative was a fairly rapid death, not necessarily a pleasant or easy one. He carefully avoided any temptation to say that he had been right and she had been wrong, or that she should have agreed to the surgery on December 1. At the same time, she put to one side her resentment over the side effects of the radiation. She would have the Gamma Knife radiation on January 17 and undergo the surgery for the two larger tumors, one old, one new, on January 25.

Not only that, but much to my surprise she finally agreed to see Dr. Jason Rubin, the oncologist Dr. Vinnie had suggested in Poughkeepsie. It was a graceful surrender on Margaret's part, although by that time it may have been too late to change anything. Then again, the difference between having the surgery in mid-December and having it on January 25 was only a matter of five weeks, which did not seem all that significant—what we failed to ask, but should have, is what the *rate of growth* of the tumors was. The cancer was, as we would soon discover, moving faster than we were, and with the failure of the radiation there was nothing to slow it down.

Margaret's decision was partly based on her trust in Alain—there was a certain *sympathie* between them, they were both stylish, attractive, and well-traveled, and most important of all Alain never lectured her. The increasing severity of Margaret's condition helped to make up her mind too: her gait was progressively more unsteady; she was taking smaller steps, she *needed* her cane now, it was no longer a prop or for difficult ground underfoot; going up and down stairs was becoming an ordeal. Her world was narrowing down day by day. She had always hated it when the cold and the short days of midwinter forced her indoors, she always preferred being outdoors walking or riding, so not surprisingly she was deeply depressed. Alain had thrown her what might be a lifeline, and to my surprise and his, she took it. I emailed Dr. Vinnie from the car on the way home and asked him if he could get an appointment with Dr. Rubin as soon as possible, before Margaret changed her mind. He replied that he would. I emailed Dawn: "Tomorrow morning Dr. Jason Rubin's secretary will call and set an appointment for Margaret for Monday at some time . . . Dr. Beltrani moved heaven and earth to get her a Monday appointment, whatever she has, take it!" This was a Thursday, and securing an appointment with a busy oncologist for Monday was above and beyond the call of friendship.

Not for the last time, I was moved by the way busy people responded to a crisis. Seen from the patient's point of view (and from that of his or her spouse) the medical world can seem like a baffling fortress, difficult to approach and remote, particularly in a major hospital, but again and again I found that, given a chance, people were eager to help and remarkably sympathetic.

The next day I thanked Alain, and he replied, "I would not have pushed for it if I did not feel it would be worth the while. Obviously, there are no guarantees, but to throw in the towel at this point would be sad."

This was exactly what I felt. I too did not want to "throw in the towel."

⁓〇

I spent the next few days, with Colleen's guidance, searching for a place where Margaret could recuperate after the surgery. At first I was disappointed: the really nice places, like the grandly named Noble Horizons, in Salisbury, Connecticut, or Woodland

Pond in New Paltz, New York, turned out to be *retirement* facilities, not for short-term rehabilitation—some of them looked so good that I was half tempted to move us both there on the spot. Who would not want an indoor heated pool and catered gourmet meals? However, I quickly realized that short-term rehabilitation was a whole different thing from assisted living. Colleen came up with the place that seemed best, the Paul Rosenthal Rehabilitation Center at Northern Dutchess Hospital, in Rhinebeck, a new, small, ten-bed facility in which each patient had a private room and bathroom. Colleen and I paid it a quick visit. Rhinebeck, more of a "destination town" with interesting shops and restaurants than Pleasant Valley, was only twenty minutes away, and we were both impressed. The rooms were big and airy, each with a private bathroom, all ten built around the horseshoe-shaped nurses' station, so there would be none of that endless ringing for a faraway and invisible nurse—if your door was open you could see them, and they could see you. There was a well-equipped gym, a dining room where those patients who were ambulatory could eat, and above all everybody we met was cheerful, willing to chat, and knowledgeable. Looking out of the window at the snow-covered fields, I said to Colleen that I would be happy to move in here myself, if I could bring a couple of books and a bottle of bourbon with me. It seemed clean, quiet, well organized, peaceful, even serene. The only problem was that because it was small it was often full, and we couldn't give them an exact date when Margaret would be discharged from WMC.

The visit to Dr. Rubin went off without any difficulty. He was attentive, sympathetic, and frank: Margaret should have a PET scan as soon as possible, after the surgery the tumors would be biopsied to see if there was a BRAF mutation, since if there *was*, there existed sophisticated treatments for melanoma despite the fairly advanced stage of Margaret's disease. He would be happy to take over Margaret's care after the surgery. He too thought Margaret should see Dr. Kluger, but understood that the *New York Times* front-page article made it unlikely that she would agree. He seemed like a very competent, reasonable man, and I felt a certain relief to have a doctor only fifteen minutes away as opposed to one or two hours away, just in case.

In case of *what*, I did not know. Both Alain and Dr. Rubin mentioned the possibility of a seizure, which sounded frightening to me once I had read up on it—there is nothing like reading about a medical subject on Wikipedia to scare the wits out of you. Would I have to put something between Margaret's teeth to prevent her from biting her tongue? With a sigh, I put it on my list of things to ask about.

As usual, the days before Margaret's surgery filled up inexorably. She needed a new medical clearance, happily arranged locally between Drs. de Lotbinière and Rubin so she did not have to go all the way down to the city and back. She also needed another blood test, and another session with Colleen to decide what she needed to pack and what I needed to buy for her. In my email to Colleen I added ". . . under a surface layer of English calm I am head over heels with anxiety," which pretty well describes it. As for Margaret, she had the kind of calm that is supposed to come over people who are about to face a firing squad, a blend of fatalism and shock. My notes from that meeting read, in part: "Chapsticks!!!! Face and body cream, toothbrush, toothpaste, toothpicks, deodorant, mouthwash, Kleenex, 2 handkerchiefs, reading glasses, Pond's Cold Cream (white, BLUE lid), Ensure? No medicines, jewelry, credit cards, cellphone." Margaret was never wholly confident of my ability to find exactly what she wanted at CVS, hence the description of the cold cream I was to look for. She had grown used to drinking a couple of bottles of Ensure a day, a diet and protein milkshake of which she liked the vanilla and chocolate flavors and hated the strawberry one. I thought she would probably get as much of what she liked as she wanted at WMC, but it never hurts to take what you like—a supply of Ensure was to become so much a part of our lives over the next three months that to this day I shudder every time I see it on a shelf at the supermarket or CVS.

I emailed Alain to tell him that Margaret's spirits were sinking very low as the date for her surgery approached, and he replied, "Nothing in life seems sufficient to prepare one for the pain of seeing a loved one suffer." We had been exchanging messages about *dukkha*, the Buddhist concept of suffering as one of the Four Noble Truths of existence, a reminder that Roseans Alain and I had a relationship that went beyond the purely medical.

Margaret and I had to get up at four in the morning to be at WMC in time for her presurgical MRI, the beginning of a long, cold, bleak day, in which I sat next to her bed holding her hand and talking about trivia until almost four o'clock in the afternoon—there was some delay about preparing the operating room. When I kissed her forehead, it was stone-cold. I saw her wheeled out on a gurney. I would not see her again until eight o'clock that night.

11.

THE SURGICAL PROCEDURE was in theory much the same as the previous one, except that it would involve two craniotomies instead of just one. Alain did the new one first, making an incision over the right parietal brain metastasis and removing a piece of the skull. "The discoloration immediately visible on the surface of the brain was evident . . . The majority of the tumor was noted to be necrotic," he noted later. In layman's terms, the tumor was enlarging fast enough to outgrow its own blood supply, and a portion of it therefore consisted of dead cells. Specimens were then taken for analysis, the tumor removed, "the cavity [in the brain] created by the melanoma" irrigated and "a cranioplasty performed," replacing the bone flap and securing it with "titanium burr hole covers and plates." Alain then turned his attention to the left frontoparietal region, from which he had debulked the tumor in April 2016 that had now returned. The scalp was incised and peeled back, the bone flap removed, the tumor immediately identified and exenterated by suction, the bone flap replaced, and a cranioplasty performed.

Brain surgery is a curious mixture of delicacy and brute force. The brain itself is the most fragile of human organs, yet opening and closing the skull requires a combination of skills somewhere between watchmaking and carpentry, involving drills, saws, burs, screwdrivers, the equivalent of pry bars, and the like, but also tiny titanium screws, latches, and pieces of mesh.

The surgery would take more than four hours—it was eight p.m. before I was able to see Margaret in her room, surrounded by high-tech equipment and looking tiny, sad, and frail, her hands carefully tied down to the bed so that she could not pluck at the tubes and wires around her. Her eyes were closed, but she was conscious and her lips were moving. I leaned over to hear what she was saying, but the only words I could distinguish were, "Why me?"

There was no good answer to that. Before her speech had become difficult or impossible to understand, Margaret would occasionally ask me if I thought she was being punished, and if so, for what? I said I didn't think so, that pain and suffering aren't dealt out according to some system of merit, they simply happen, but although Margaret disliked all forms of religion—no doubt the legacy of those years in a convent school, baths in cold water and discipline administered by the nuns with a ruler—she nevertheless wanted to believe that there was some orderly system, that somebody was keeping score. An accidental explanation, that things just *happen*, that nobody is in charge, did not satisfy her, nor did a cause-and-effect explanation—after all, plenty of people spent just as much time in the sun as Margaret had, life was full of women in the 1960s and 1970s who associated a year-round tan with glamour, yet most of them did not end up in a hospital bed after two brain surgeries and two different kinds of radiation.

"Why me?" is a good question, but not an answerable one, and I sensibly held her hand instead of trying. Her eyelids occasionally fluttered, she knew I was there, and sometimes being there is the most you can do, all that is needed. When I left for the night I emailed Dawn, "Margaret is in her room, plugged into wires and tubes, very miserable . . . very restless. Terrible . . . Dr. DL removed (or "debulked") two tumors, but thinks Margaret will need further treatment, Gamma Knife radiation, possibly some form of chemo. Path forward not going to be easy."

The next day made that clear. Margaret's restlessness had increased, her speech had improved slightly, but she was in a state of extreme high anxiety about her horses and cats, all of which were of course being looked after perfectly well. I emailed a reply to Megan's message asking how Margaret was: "Today very difficult, she's very tired and distracted about cats, and how much they are being fed. I said Tiz Whiz [the barn cat] doing fine, but she wanted to know how much [she had eaten], of what, and what happens if we run out of it." It did no good for me to assure Margaret that we had an ample supply of Fancy Feast Marinated Tuna Morsels, or that in the unlikely event we ran out of it Megan could pick up more at the supermarket; she wanted an exact count of the number of cans we had left. Margaret passed the day hyperfocusing on the care of her animals while I soothed and reassured her as much as I could, to no avail. At the end of the day I emailed our friend Linda Fountain, "Not a good day, speech still very difficult, mind distracted, but she did eat (with my help) half a tuna sandwich cut into little pieces . . . In Neuro-ICU she has her own nurse 24 hours a day, which helps. I have put social worker here in touch with Northern Dutchess Hospital Acute Care, so hopefully she can go to Paul Rosenthal Rehabilitation Center by ambulance on discharge. One step at a time."

I was beginning to feel the effects of pressure, Margaret's anxiety level was hard to deal with—it was not *her*, I told myself, it was the disease, the surgery, the swelling of the brain as it reacted to what had been done to it; but still, after a couple of hours of repeating that she should not be worrying, that we had plenty of cat food (or hay, or whatever), it *felt* like criticism, and by seven p.m., when the Neuro-ICU nurse shooed me out despite Margaret's agonizing pleas for me to stay, I had to sit down outside the hospital in the cold for a few minutes of deep breathing before the long drive home, where I would arrive around nine o'clock, pour myself a glass of bourbon, feed the cats, then warm up my dinner, knowing I would have to do it all over again the next day. Do not mistake me, I do not compare any of that to what Margaret was going through, but the "caregiver," to use a favorite term in the kind of leaflets hospitals pass out, has his or her own pressures to deal with, among them guilt (Why her and not me?), fear, fatigue, and occasionally anger, which of course adds to the guilt.

Colleen's big, cheerful husband Ray Greco owns the Corner Deli only a mile or so away from us, and always has on hand a Reese's Peanut Butter and chocolate chip cookie that Margaret particularly liked, so Colleen and her daughter Megan made sure I had a daily supply of them to bring down to WMC, as well as meatballs to eat when I got home. When all else failed I would break the cookie into tiny pieces and feed it to her a bit at a time, washed down slowly with a bottle of chocolate Ensure. She ate more of that than the hospital food, but it was still not much.

Two days after the surgery I was able to tell Alain, "Margaret seems slightly better today than yesterday . . . Yesterday she was saying she wished she was dead, but a bit more upbeat today. Physical therapist got her up and walking a bit—he was very good, remembered her from last time." This was not so surprising—Margaret's physical therapists always remembered her, she excelled at the exercises and loved doing them. It was the one part of the process of recovery and rehabilitation that she looked forward to.

Alain replied, "Saw Margaret this morning, sleeping like an angel, so I did not wake her! MRI fine, no surprises. Discharge M/Tu still on." Margaret was convinced that the sooner she was discharged from WMC, the sooner she would get better. She did not like her nurses as much as she had liked the ones on her previous stay in the Neuro-ICU, and, far from being a restful place in which to recover, this time it gave the impression of a busy train station, bells constantly ringing, people waking her up the moment she fell asleep. Despite all the medications and every effort on my part, her anxiety and irritability spiked. Ready or not, she wanted out, and longed for her departure. Unfortunately, despite all the arrangements for her to be transferred on Monday, January 30, there was a last-minute glitch. Northern Dutchess didn't have a bed for her yet, so she had to stay until Tuesday. "Let's hope everything will be smooth sailing for tomorrow," Alain wrote, but that too turned out to be more difficult than anticipated.

"Long, bad day here," I wrote Linda, "Margaret did NOT go to Rhinebeck Rehabilitation this morning, at the last minute they didn't have a bed free, so she's stuck [here], exhausted, stick-thin, depressed and anxious, all hair gone, keeps saying that she wishes she were dead . . . I understand that, but I am hoping we will get her to Rhinebeck by ambulance tomorrow, and that we will have a chance [there] to reconnect her to life."

The next morning nature intervened with a sudden, blinding blizzard. I was so busy dealing with all the paperwork needed for Margaret's discharge that I did not notice it until we got her gurney down to the ambulance loading dock. There was a thick layer of snow everywhere, the parking lot was almost empty, and nothing seemed to be moving on the roads. It was snowing fiercely. The crew of the ambulance I had hired was looking skeptical. The distance between WMC and Rhinebeck is about seventy-five miles, an hour-and-a-half drive in good weather. It was not good weather. "This don't look good," the driver of the ambulance said. "And it's worse farther north," his partner added. "Going to be a hell of a storm. Taconic Parkway might be closed any minute."

I looked at Margaret lying on the gurney behind the glass doors. She was covered in blankets and her own coat, her head swathed in bandages as if she were wearing a turban, with only her small, white face showing. I could tell from her eyes that what she was saying, or at least thinking, was: *Get me out of here!*

There was a bed waiting for her right now in Rhinebeck. I sighed. "Guys," I said, "we *have* to get her to Northern Dutchess. Please." They stared at the snow. Visibility was near-zero, strong winds blew the snow in our faces, stinging like hail. I could see they both thought I was crazy.

"What if they close the Taconic on us?" the driver asked.

"That's what you've got flashing lights and a siren for, surely," I said, more sharply than I had intended.

"That's for an emergency," he said.

"You don't understand, this *is* an emergency." I paused. "I'll tell you what, I have a friend who's a cop, I'll give him a call and he may be able to help. On top of that, one hundred dollars each when we get her to Northern Dutchess. Is that a deal?"

They looked at each other and shrugged. "Let's load her up," the driver said. While they slid Margaret and all her gear into the ambulance and secured her, I dialed my friend on his personal cell phone. He was a shooting buddy; when he was doing K-9 training Margaret had always allowed him to work his dog on our land. By luck I got him on patrol and explained the problem. They were right, he said, the Taconic was about to be shut down tight as a drum, but an ambulance would probably get away with it, and anyway he would swing down and meet us halfway and escort us in.

I passed this good news on to the ambulance guys, and with

Margaret strapped and wired up to the monitors, lights flashing, we crept through the streets of Valhalla and swung onto the Taconic Parkway, which was absolutely deserted—even the snowplows weren't out yet. I was sitting in front next to the driver, and I could only see Margaret by turning my head around until the muscles in my neck hurt. Her eyes were shut. The other member of the crew sat next to her on a folding seat, checking her vitals on the monitors and talking to her soothingly. These guys were pros, I could see.

I could hardly even make out the side of the road or the guardrails. Apart from the occasional mild skid we progressed at a fairly steady pace, although it was as dark as night. Every once in a while we passed a snowplow as we headed north, but most of the time the parkway ahead was as pristine as a ski slope, no tire tracks on it at all. The snowplows pulled over to let us pass at the sight of the flashing lights coming up behind them. The driver kept both hands firmly on the wheel, and a gentle foot for the brake and accelerator. Up in our part of the country a gift for driving in the snow is not only useful, but much admired— Margaret's ability to get back and forth from our farm to Rhinebeck to have her nails done driving her Porsche 911 in even the heaviest of snowstorms won her as much admiration locally as her horsemanship—more, in fact. "You're good at this," I said.

"I was a driver in the Tenth Mountain Division."

I nodded. "Up at Fort Drum?"

He gave me a brief look. "It snows six months a year up there, over ten feet a year." I said I knew, that's why they put the mountain division up there in the first place.

"You're a veteran?" he asked.

"Well, yes, I suppose so, but not here. I was in the Royal Air Force, a lifetime ago." It's one of those odd things about American life, military service of any kind generates a degree of respect not found anywhere else. Nobody in England would have asked the question, or cared about the answer one way or the other. "My buddy back there was in the Air Force," the driver said, and explained to the EMT in the back over the intercom that I had been an airman too. The EMT gave me a thumbs-up. The storm was much worse now, all traces of the roadway obliterated, and I would not have been surprised if the driver had pulled off the parkway to wait it out, but now that my status as a veteran had been established, he appeared determined to go on. You don't let a fellow veteran down.

Just before the exit to Interstate 84 I could see the blue and red flashing lights of a police car, a four-wheel drive vehicle of some kind, which pulled out and led us all the way to the Rhinebeck exit, just as promised. For a moment I was completely disoriented—this was not the direction from which I usually approached Rhinebeck, and the snow made everything seem ghostly and unfamiliar, like the winter scene in *Dr. Zhivago*. I wondered if we had come this far only to get lost, but before I could ask whether he knew the way, we had pulled into the emergency room dock. Two nurses were waiting to move Margaret with a gurney. I had thought she was asleep or sedated, but apparently not. She looked at the snow and shook her head. "Way to go, guys," she said quite clearly, before the nurses wheeled her away. "She drives a Porsche 911 in the snow?" the EMT said. "Gutsy lady." Evidently she had been talking to the EMT. I said she was indeed, gave them each a hundred-dollar bill. We shook hands solemnly, and I followed Margaret into the building carrying the Vuitton bag that had accompanied her all over the world.

Her room looked out over snow-covered fields. It was cheery, airy, decorated in soothing colors, quiet, almost serene. She was already in bed. On one wall was a whiteboard showing the schedule for the next week, every day already filled up with speech, physical, and occupational therapy. On the night table beside the bed was a telephone, a welcome sign of normality, since patients in the Neuro-ICU did not get a telephone—they were mostly in no state to use one.

I emailed Alain to tell him we had arrived safely, and he emailed back, "Wonderful news! Bravo." Her internist, Dr. Adam, emailed from New York City, "Please know Margaret is in our prayers." People complain about the indifference of doctors in these days when every practice is becoming part of a larger medical entity, but Margaret's doctors took as warm an interest in her as her friends. While she dozed, I caught up on my emails, and replied to one from Lynn Nesbit, my best friend and agent for over forty years and my number-one morale-booster: "Ghastly journey by ambulance up the Taconic through a blizzard. I hope she will be more comfortable [here] and perhaps come home in about ten days to two weeks. Outlook hard to say. Probably chemo for melanoma, a whole new treatment but with very risky side effects. Surgery and radiation have gone about as far as they can go."

Margaret settled down quickly into the routine at the Paul Rosenthal Rehabilitation Center. She didn't want visitors, except for Colleen—she was embarrassed about the way she looked—but she began to take telephone calls from Megan and from Miguel, and to reconnect with news about the farm. Her anxiety level dropped as long as she was kept busy. Each landmark meant a lot to her. Five days after her arrival, her sutures were removed; the next day her hair was washed, what little she still had of it. Not surprisingly, she longed to be home.

Except for breakfast, about which I could do nothing because visiting hours didn't begin until eleven a.m., I took care of food. At noon, I stopped at Ray's deli on the way over to Rhinebeck and bought her an egg-salad sandwich and an order of crisp bacon for lunch, and a Reese's peanut butter cookie for tea. In the evening,

I asked Rob to bring in either the crab cake appetizer from the Tavern at the Beekman Arms, a pizza margherita from Gigi's, or fried baby artichokes with garlic mayonnaise from Terrapin—Rhinebeck probably has more (and more varied) restaurants per head of population than any other small town in New York State—or whatever else I thought she might like. Eating was still difficult for her, everything had to be cut up into minuscule pieces (I carried a sharp knife in a scabbard on my belt for just that purpose), and her appetite remained very poor; still, at least she was eating *something*.

Her leftovers were usually enough for my own dinner, and I took to bringing in a screw-top jar full of white wine marked with Margaret's name on a piece of white surgical tape and put it with the urine samples in the refrigerator outside the room. I wasn't too sure how the nurses would react to a bottle of Cloudy Bay New Zealand Chardonnay there, but the jar didn't attract any attention.

She was still frightened and lonely, but a deluge of emails from friends kept her interested, although her spirits plummeted on Sunday, when there was no therapy. "The hospital at Rhinebeck is fine," I emailed Linda, "much better than Burke or WMC, only ten patients, but she is going stir-crazy." She loved messages that reconnected her with her world, like one from Carol Kozlowski, who had just been made president of the United States Eventing Association (the governing body of Margaret's sport). Carol had been seated next to the great British Olympic gold medalist William Fox-Pitt, MBE at the annual meeting. He told Carol about his terrible fall in 2015 that put him in a coma for two weeks, and said he still suffered from memory loss and would burst into tears for no reason. Carol went off to deal with the paperwork that would make her presidency official and realized too late that she had slipped Fox-Pitt's notes for his speech into her briefcase just as he was starting to speak. "In a brief deer-in-the-headlights moment, I had visions of William coming to a halt in his speech and bursting into tears . . . I thought to myself, 'Good God, I've been President for 5 minutes and I've already torpedoed William Fox-Pitt!' "

When she read that it was the first time I had heard Margaret laugh for many weeks, a good, hearty belly laugh as she imagined the scene—how she would have liked to been there!—but there was still no way she could reply except to dictate to me, the fingers of her right hand were useless.

Margaret's occupational therapy concentrated on getting her fingers to work again. This was perhaps the tensest hour of her day, as she tried to pick up square pegs and put them in square holes and the round ones in round holes, her face a study of concentration—and all too often, frustration—as the piece fell from her fingers or she was unable to put them in the right holes. Physical therapy, as usual, went well, speech therapy much less well, but we also spent at least a couple of hours a day walking around the hospital, Margaret using her walker. I dressed her twice a day for her walks. Once, as I put her running shoes on, I said, "I haven't tied the laces on anybody else's shoes since Chris was a little boy. I'm learning how to tie your laces at about the same time in my life as I'm forgetting how to tie my own!"

Northern Dutchess is small, as hospitals go (eighty-four beds), but once we left the rehabilitation center and turned right, the corridors wound on for what seemed like miles, intersecting with each other so that it was easy to get lost. From time to time we would confront a locked door to an operating room or radiation and have to backtrack, but in time we began to recognize enough landmarks to guide us back and to give us a good idea of how far we had been walking. There were occasional sitting areas, or banks of potted palms, and at one point a window that gave a good view toward the snow-covered Catskills. Soon some of the patients and staff began to recognize us, Margaret in the baseball cap she wore to events with a message embroidered on the front that read "Born to Cowboy," a pair of old worn blue jeans that hung loosely on her because she had lost so much weight, and a navy-blue hoodie with her "Team Stonegate Farm" logo. There was something gallant and determined about her as she walked through the maze of hospital corridors. Patients who saw her from their beds gave her a thumbs-up as she passed, and so did the nurses and doctors along the way. When she got back to her room she was exhausted, but movement buoyed her spirits— there was no way she could lie in bed and watch television, she never turned it on once.

I was already making plans for her to repeat her rehabilitation exercises at MidHudson Hospital, and to arrange for Chris Dayger to be her physical therapist again. Alain had set her next MRI for six weeks away and we had made another appointment for her to see Dr. Jason Rubin, which Margaret was already sorry she had agreed to.

Exactly two weeks after she had arrived at Northern Dutchess Hospital Margaret was discharged. I reported to Alain that the doctor had been very impressed by the amount of progress she had made, but warned her sternly that she should not ride or drive for several months because of the risk of a seizure. I pointed out to Alain that it would be hard to keep her off a horse, and probably unkind.

He also warned Margaret she should not drink. Margaret was not a big drinker, I pointed out, but one weakish vodka tonic before dinner was a comforting part of her routine. Alain replied promptly that these were standard recommendations after brain surgery, but added: "I tend to individualize my recommendations. As I am not really worried that Margaret is going to finish off an entire bottle of vodka, I do not think we should deprive her of her vodka tonic before a meal, especially if it helps to stimulate her appetite!" A doctor after my own heart!

Margaret's return home was uneventful. She visited her horses, pushing her walker through the snow, but making it upstairs in the house was more difficult than ever, even with me coming behind her to make sure she didn't fall. I had clipped an ad for a stair lift from a magazine, and made a mental note to see about putting one in. Margaret would certainly resist making such a major alteration to the house, but we might still have to do it, I decided. I had purchased a bath lift, so that if or when we needed it we would be able to put it in.

But once again I had underestimated the speed at which the disease moves.

12.

SEEING MARGARET RIDE every morning again gave me the impression that she was back to normal, but that was an illusion. Of course she was riding within a week, not for long rides, just walking the horse, but still, back in the saddle. She loved riding in the snow, and there was plenty of it. Our paint horse Monty liked it too, he would have seen plenty of snow growing up in Montana.

Taking her daily walk was a more difficult proposition, since there were big snowbanks on both sides of the roads and it was discouragingly cold; cars came hurtling down the narrow road, so you constantly had to worry about one of them skidding on a patch of ice and running into you. It was my assistant Dawn who suggested we try the Galleria, the big shopping mall on Route 9 in Poughkeepsie, as a place to walk indoors.

I am not much of a mall person myself, but Margaret could spend an hour or two there shopping quite happily. If I went with her I usually brought the *New York Times* with me and sat reading it and drinking a cappuccino while she shopped.

Margaret took to walking in the Galleria at once. After we had ridden I would drive her there in the morning, park the car at the northern end of the mall outside Macy's—at eleven in the morning the parking lot was virtually empty, as was the mall itself—then walk all the way through the mall to the southern far end, as far as you could go down the aisles of cookware and toys at Target. To avoid boredom, we sometimes took the escalator up to the second floor for the walk back. At a rough guess a complete circuit added up to a little less than a mile, if we added a swing through the endless aisles of sports clothes in Dick's Sporting Goods, and it took Margaret about half an hour using her walker, a little less once she had graduated to a cane. I could judge our progress by the counters or shops we passed. Once we had passed the Macy's perfume counter we were in the long aisle of the mall proper; the halfway point was Aéropostale, and at the far end of the toy counters in Target there was a wall where we turned around and headed for home.

The mall always reminded me in width and length of airstrips I had flown from in the Second Tactical Air Force of the British Army of the Rhine, except for the terrazzo and faux-marble flooring and the kiosks selling pretzels or offering while-you-wait cell phone repair. On the upper floor Bare Essentials was our halfway point, and Francesca's Collections meant that we were approaching Macy's again, where we took the escalator down and walked through the store past the women's underwear and stockings to the exit at the far end, where we were parked. Within a few days we were recognized as regulars. There were people who jogged every morning in the mall during the winter, and of course people opening the shops and setting up the counters. The young man baking his first batch of pretzels of the day always gave us a cheery greeting, but most of the indoor joggers were too self-involved to bother, or perhaps frightened by the sight of somebody using a walker. People exercising always want to believe that fitness will spare them from this kind of thing. By now I knew better.

We came to believe that the mall belonged to us. It was cavernous and almost empty first thing in the morning, with the smell of things cooking in the food court and everything looking bright and clean. As the days went by, Margaret increased the distance and the speed. She was determined that I time us and write down the results every day, as if she were training for an Olympic event, so I carried a little notebook and a pencil in my pocket for that purpose. She was cramming a lot into every day—riding, her walk in the Galleria, physical and speech therapy—not so surprisingly by teatime she was exhausted. Climbing the stairs for her bath wiped her out, the bath itself was still an ordeal for both of us. She managed to come downstairs in her bathrobe for her drink and dinner, but she did not eat much.

After the second week of walking in the mall I began to notice that very slowly, day by day, Margaret was beginning to list ever so slightly to her right, so I occasionally had to take her arm to support her. It did not slow her down, she did not even seem to be aware she was doing it, but then one morning, quite suddenly, on the way back to Macy's, she fell to her right, and for an instant I thought she was going to crash through the plate-glass window of Bath & Body Works. I managed to catch her just in time. She had a hard time getting up again, but a total stranger rushed over and took her other arm, and together we put her back on her feet again. She was unsteady and disoriented.

"Can you walk back to the car?" I asked. She shook her head. We were near a side entrance, so I asked the man if we could get her seated in the Macy's shoe department, would he mind staying with her while I brought the car around? He said he would be happy to, so I ran through Macy's, got the car, and left it parked as close as I could to the side exit with the engine running, and together we carried her to the car, put her in, and fastened her seat belt.

Sitting in an idling car in the parking lot of a shopping mall is not the ideal place to talk about dying, but then what place is?

"Is this the beginning of the end?" she asked calmly.

"It's not a good sign."

"Was it a seizure, do you think? Dr. Rubin mentioned seizures."

Margaret's consultation with Dr. Rubin had gone smoothly enough, although he mentioned that Mayo Clinic tests on the specimen harvested by Dr. Alain from the older tumor had failed to identify a BRAF mutation that might have made treatment for advanced melanoma possible. That was not good news, though I'm not sure it sank in. Both of us liked Dr. Rubin, he had a certain low-key authority disguised by a gentle manner, as if he were saying, *Look, I'm sorry, but this is the way it is.* Those were not his exact words, but that was the message conveyed.

Further radiation was unlikely to help; chemotherapy would be ineffective against the brain tumors; immunotherapy, whether at Yale–New Haven or elsewhere, was the next step, the *only* step. But Margaret did not want to become "a pincushion," as she put it, meaning to become a patient in a trial of experimental drugs, in and out of emergency rooms and living with side effects. Dr. Rubin was not about to give us a timetable for the progression of the disease, nor did we expect one. Margaret respected him, but all her instincts were against following his advice. I had mixed feelings. If it were me, I would probably have chosen to try a more aggressive treatment, but at the same time I understood and respected Margaret's feelings—after all, she was the one with brain cancer, not me. I anticipated that I would feel guilty about not pushing her harder, but my guilt feelings were my problem, not hers.

"I don't think it was a seizure," I said to her, since I had been reading up on them. I put the car in drive; there was no point to sitting in the parking lot. A seizure sounded like a recognizable and very much more terrifying event—this had been more of a slow, stately roll toward the floor, something beyond her control, but not sudden or violent.

"This is all happening faster than I thought," she said.

"It probably doesn't help that you're pushing yourself so hard, you know. You're tired, you're not giving yourself a chance to rest."

Margaret did not look convinced by this; I wasn't myself, although I thought an occasional rest couldn't hurt. "I don't want to be sent away somewhere to die," she said. "Don't do that."

"Okay." I felt some unease. This was something somebody, perhaps Colleen, had suggested—that I should look into the Kaplan Family Hospice Residence across the river in Newburgh, which had a reputation as the best hospice in the Mid-Hudson area. I had looked it up on the internet. I thought of it as something to keep in mind in the long term, if or when push came to shove, not something in the immediate future. It was small— eleven beds, each with a bathroom, a view of the gardens and small terrace—and looked as serene and comfortable as a place to die could be. Of course, it was a well-orchestrated sales pitch, with beautiful photography, smiling, caring faces, and soothing background music; still, even allowing for all that, it seemed like a good choice. Unrestricted visiting hours, including pets, and a "professional on-site chef manager" sounded promising, although I did not imagine that Margaret would benefit from "spiritual care" or use the meditation room. Kaplan did not accept people until they had less than six months to live, and many of their patients arrived in the last days of their life. We had no way of knowing at this point into which category Margaret might fall, but it was clear enough from the expression on her face that she was not going there until she was helpless or unconscious, if then, so I put it out of my mind. Whatever was coming, I would have to deal with it myself at home, rather than moving her to Newburgh to be cared for.

I did not think I could have done that anyway. Nothing had puzzled Margaret more than the fact that when her mother was clearly beginning to sink into senile dementia her father put Kit in a nursing home, and never once visited her there. Margaret was her father's daughter, much more like Paul in every way than like her gentle mother Kit, but even so, from time to time she would ask why, *how* could Paul have done that, and ask me to promise not to. I always thought of this as a rhetorical question; I was older, Margaret's mind was as sharp as a tack, I had always assumed that she was much more likely to be looking after me and thinking about putting *me* in a nursing home than the other way around. But here we were, exactly where we had never expected to be.

I realized now that if she was going to stay at home, I had a lot of changes to make. Some of them were minor, others more ambitious, like putting in the stair lift, a shower, or a state-of-the-art toilet, things that were in the nature of long-term projects. That there might not *be* a long term had not yet fully dawned on me.

With the help of Colleen and other friends I began to put together a list of local people who were reliable professional care-givers. Margaret was still determined not to have anybody living in the house, but she might put up with somebody coming in during the day to help look after her. I made a mental note to ask Thom Schwartz, who had lived down the road from us for over twenty years—I remembered that he and his wife were nurses—if he could recommend someone. I did not see all this as something that was immediately necessary, it was more a question of getting prepared for the future.

I was wrong.

***

There was no repetition of Margaret's fall at the Galleria and we rearranged her schedule to give her time for an afternoon nap every day, which did indeed help some. Her hairdresser Tom emailed from New York that he had taken a photograph of her over to the wigmaker so that she would have a wig that exactly duplicated her hair when it was at its best, that is to say, after he had just done it. On February 27 she had her first postoperative consultation with Alain, who felt she was "recovering well" from surgery. He noticed the occasional word-finding difficulty, but he remarked that her speech had improved since the surgery. She was to continue on a small dose of dexamethasone to inhibit any swelling in the brain, and stay on Keppra to prevent seizures. We were sufficiently buoyed by that to order dinner in from nearby Joseph's Steakhouse in Hyde Park, a quiet oasis of dark wood in the New York City steakhouse tradition, more or less dedicated to the memory of Frank Sinatra. Margaret's favorite meal was a filet mignon with béarnaise sauce and onion rings, fresh asparagus béarnaise, and Joseph's famous peanut-butter-and-raspberry torte, the last a present to us from Joseph. Of course, everything had to be cut up into tiny pieces for Margaret, and she didn't eat much of it, but what she ate, she enjoyed. I opened a bottle of 2012 Napa Valley Waypoint and we clinked glasses.

***

Only a week later Margaret had another serious fall, this time while brushing her teeth in the evening. She slipped over to the right and before I could reach her she was trapped between the sink and the toilet, bleeding from several lacerations on her leg. Again, it was not a seizure—she simply began to list slowly like a ship rolling over and was unable to stop it. This was not a violent fall, but her skin was by now so fragile that the slightest impact could draw blood. Although her weight was down to 106 pounds, Margaret was not easy to lift from her predicament, since she was wedged into a narrow space and I worried about hurting her more. She was bleeding profusely now, but perfectly conscious. "I'm ruining the bath mat," she said, quite clearly. I thought that was the least of our problems. I called our barn manager Miguel, who came over at once with his wife Maria, and the three of us managed to extricate Margaret from where she had fallen, then take her to the emergency room at MidHudson Hospital to have her wounds stitched up, the first of several visits there. I had no particular reason to choose MidHudson over Vassar—they were both about the same distance away—but Margaret had been coming to MidHudson daily for her physical therapy, so it was on our flight path.

In the ER, as I filled out the list of the medications that Margaret was taking, it occurred to me that her falls might to some degree be explained by what she was on, although that would prove to be wishful thinking. The list included acetaminophen-oxycodone, allopurinol, 100mg; aripiprazole, 2mg; atropine-diphenoxylate, 2.5mg; clonazepam, 0.5mg; conjugated estrogens, 0.3mg; fluconazole, 150mg; Keppra, lorazepam, 2mg; lovastatin, 20mg; naproxen, 500mg; progesterone, 200mg; and Venlafaxine, 50mg.

A quick look on my cell phone at the possible side effects of Keppra alone was enough to make me nervous—they ran the gamut from suicidal thoughts and paranoia to vomiting and double vision, and that's without even considering how all these medications might interact with each other. The ER doctor raised an eyebrow as she read this list. "Has she been on all these a long time?"

"Except for Keppra and a couple of others, yes, most of them for years," I explained.

"Did this happen before or after she took the clonazepam and the lorazepam?"

"Before. I give her those when she's in bed, with a little Ensure or warm milk."

She shrugged. "Then it's probably all right, I don't think they have anything to do with her fall."

Margaret was quite comfortable in the ER. Colleen and Megan had come over, so there were a few of us clustered around her bed as the doctor glued up her wounds (no surprises there, horse vets had been using Krazy Glue instead of sutures for years) and a very nice male nurse with extraordinarily elaborate tattoos that covered every visible square inch of skin gently bandaged her legs and tended to her rehydration drip. Unlike most ERs, which are busy, noisy places, this one was quiet and restful; in fact, Margaret dozed comfortably. I tucked this observation in the back of my mind just in case—God forbid!—we needed an ER again. By midnight she was back home in bed sleeping, with one leg elevated on a pillow as instructed.

It was soon apparent that Margaret's lacerations took a lot longer to heal than with earlier wounds. The dressings had to be changed frequently. Colleen came over to show me how to do it, but there was never any chance of my being able to match the speed and neatness with which she changed a dressing. Whether it was the effect of the cancer or the radiation, Margaret's skin was now extraordinarily fragile, bruises appeared for no reason and refused to heal. Nevertheless, over the next few days Margaret carried on as before, riding Monty and exercising, although I now held on to her arm much more tightly in the Galleria and tried to keep her in the dead center of the mall so there was no danger of her falling into a plate-glass window.

I did not want to be distracted from looking after Margaret by any health problems of my own, but I had recently lost almost all the hearing in my right ear. I supposed that my hearing aids were at fault—no device is more temperamental, never mind how much they cost—and found time to fit in a visit to my audiologist, who found there was nothing wrong with my hearing aids, and, having given me a hearing test, rushed me in to see Dr. Jason Cohen at once. Since it is usually difficult to get an appointment with Dr. Cohen in a hurry, this was enough to warn me that I was not about to hear good news. And so it proved: a sudden, precipitous loss of hearing in one ear can result, I learned, from an acoustic neuroma, a tumor growing on the cranial nerves that connect the ear to the brain.

The appropriate treatment for it was brain surgery to debulk the tumor, and the first step was to have an MRI, for which he wrote me a prescription. It occurred to me at once that two people recovering from brain surgery in one house was likely to prove very difficult. On the way home I called Alain, my go-to now for all such questions, who reassured me that in the event that an acoustic neuroma was diagnosed (extremely unlikely) brain surgery might not be necessary. He had taken care of many acoustic neuromas with Gamma Knife radiation as the sole treatment, I should not let it worry me. Then I called my electrocardiologist Jeffrey Matos in the city, always a kindly and sensible listener, and he pointed out that I couldn't have an MRI anyway because of my implanted pacemaker-defibrillator.

I metaphorically slapped myself on the head—of *course* I should have remembered that! I called Dr. Cohen, who put me on dexamethasone instead to see if that would reduce any swelling, so Margaret and I were now on some of the same medication. As it turned out, the dexamethasone worked over time, and my hearing gradually returned to what it had been—not great, but sufficient. I told Margaret I was suffering from an ear infection, there was no point in burdening her with another medical drama at this point in her life, but it brought home to me how dependent Margaret was on me as her only caregiver. I had no backup if anything went wrong. Even a fall from my horse or a bad case of flu would create a real problem.

These worries were borne out only a couple of weeks later, when another fall, this time in the kitchen, gashed Margaret's leg open almost to the bone. She lost so much blood that I called 911, and knelt next to her until the Pleasant Valley Fire Department ambulance arrived, trying to stanch the blood with one hand and hold her hand with the other. The ambulance arrived promptly, the crew consisting of three familiar faces from Dunkin' Donuts, plus a Dutchess County deputy sheriff who arrived at the same time. They were all efficient, kind, caring, and professional. The staff at the MidHudson ER were surprised to see Margaret back so soon, but once again they patched her up efficiently and she was home in bed by midnight.

It was apparent to me now that I needed help, despite Margaret's reluctance to have a stranger in the house.

PART III

"Field of Dreams."

13.

THIS TIME THE damage to Margaret's leg was more serious. It was heavily bandaged, which made getting her in and out of bed and walking much more difficult. "I think you're going to need help," she finally said to me, at last opening the way for a nurse to come in during the day. She still did not want a live-in nurse installed in one of the guest rooms, although as we would soon discover it is the nighttime when bad things usually happen, particularly when it's necessary to help the patient out of bed and get her to the bathroom and back. It was typical of Margaret to say that *I* needed help, not she. She shied away from anything that suggested weakness or fear on her part.

Still, we had made a step forward. On Dan Scharff's recommendation I interviewed Laura Sanders, an attractive, bright, energetic RN with over thirty years of hospital experience, who was now doing private home care. She and her husband lived only ten minutes from our farm, and better still, she and Margaret took to each other immediately. That freed me to start in on what we needed to do in the house. With Dan's help I persuaded Acorn Stairlifts to put in a stair lift in one day, with the minimum of noise or a fuss, so Margaret would be almost unaware that it was going in. I also gave the bath lift a trial run, without much success.

Also important, I found, thanks to Colleen, a couple of backups for Laura, which gave us nurse care seven days a week during the day, and with all that arranged I began to explore the possibility of home hospice care, *just in case*, as I told myself. But events were now moving rapidly—so rapidly that it was hard to mistake them for anything but the warning signs of much worse to come.

Keeping up a cheerful spirit of optimism toward those one loves is an English character trait, a Panglossian gene built into my DNA, no doubt inherited from my insanely cheerful actress mother, who would have said to a corpse, *Oh, cheer up, darling, you'll be better in no time.* "The show must go on" was my mother's motto, she believed it was her duty to be bright and vivacious, and perhaps selfishly she looked upon other people's lack of happiness as an attack on her own. Margaret was not quite so determined to put a cheerful face on things, but she too was not one to let anyone she knew wallow in grief, still less herself. "Buck up!" was what her father would tell her if she was in low spirits or had a fall from a horse; he did not lavish sympathy on his daughter, or anyone else. But at some point, I was beginning to recognize, realism is kinder. Margaret was still going out daily to the tack room leaning on her walker to have coffee and check up on her horses, but by now she was no longer able to mount the patient Monty, even with Miguel helping her up the three steps of the mounting block and into the saddle.

She could no longer write herself, of course, but on February 25, 2017, in the diary in the tack room, in which everything to do with the horses had to be recorded, Megan wrote, in capitals, "MARGARET'S LAST RIDE."

Less than eight days after Margaret's latest visit to the ER I had to call for an ambulance again, this time at ten o'clock at night—

Margaret was suffering quite suddenly from acute shortness of breath, her heartbeat was alarmingly high even to my untutored touch, her ankles were swollen with fluid, she was gasping as if she were drowning, her speech was garbled and desperate. Once again, the ambulance came swiftly, and once again we were greeted in the MidHudson ER as if we were old friends, but this time there was a perceptible change of atmosphere. Margaret was being treated like someone who was in serious trouble. We no longer had a problem, we had a crisis.

A doctor appeared at once. Margaret was put on oxygen and an IV hydration drip the moment she was in her room. An EKG was taken, she was attached to monitors, and we—the usual cast, myself, Miguel, Maria, Colleen, and Megan—were asked to leave the room while Margaret watched us go with wild, staring eyes. It took some time before the doctor was able to emerge and tell us that Margaret's breathing and heartbeat were under control and she was resting peacefully. As soon as she was stabilized she would be taken for a "CT angiography chest with intravenous contrast," to see what was going on.

Ironically, Margaret was about to have, now that she was no longer in any position to resist, the CT/PET scan that she had been putting off. The results confirmed the presence of two growing tumors in her lungs, enough to suggest that the edema in her legs and the shortness of breath were caused by the spread of tumors in her body.

A few days later, when she next saw Alain for a new MRI, his notes reflected the unmistakable deterioration in her condition. He saw a distinct decrease in the coordination of her right hand and "some increased difficulties with regard to her speech," as well as an unsteady gait. There was evidence of "residual/recurrent tumor within the two resection cavities, with a corresponding increase in mass effect"—in other words, the tumors were once again pressing against the brain tissue in the tightly confined space of the skull. Alain told us all this in terms that Margaret could not misunderstand, and urged her to discuss the option of palliative immunotherapy or chemotherapy with Dr. Rubin, adding, in his letter to Dr. Rubin: "She has indicated to me that she is not interested in pursuing any additional radiation therapy, which is quite understandable given its failure to control the larger two metastases. She may also decide at this point that she does not wish to pursue either chemotherapy or immunotherapy, in the end it is her decision to make."

Margaret's speech was in decline. She was beginning to have troubles with the fingers of her *left* hand as well as those of her right, a sign that the tumor on the right side of her brain was growing again. But her determination not to pursue further treatment remained unchanged. Alain was right, it *was* her decision to make, and she was making it, as she always did—after all, doing nothing is doing something, in every life decision. She was not in any way suicidal, she had simply concluded that nothing on offer from Dr. Rubin, or even from Alain, was going to give her back the life she wanted or turn her back into the person she had been. She didn't like it, she was as afraid of death as most of us are, she did not believe in an afterlife of any kind—Margaret had simply looked into the future and seen nothing there she wanted. She did not propose to "go gentle into that good night," and from time to time summoned up the energy to "rage against the dying of the light," to quote from Dylan Thomas, one of her favorite poets. Anger, fear, and anxiety consumed her in ebbs and waves, but she struggled to keep them under control, her father's daughter to the end. Most of the time she was placid, exhausted by the slightest physical effort; at other times, unpredictably, rage suddenly gripped her, filling her with a brief burst of energy in which she shouted over and over again, "Who is to blame for this?" Sometimes she blamed me, sometimes the doctors, sometimes fate, sometimes people whose names I didn't always recognize. *Someone*, she would repeat, fists clenched, her face distorted with anger, must be to blame for all this, someone would have to pay. Then, as the effort drained her, the rage subsided and she fell quiet again. It was not comfortable to be the target of her rage, but I recognized the impulse—when terrible things happen to us, we all need to blame someone, usually the person who is closest. Strangely, it was in these outbursts that Margaret seemed most like her old self, energetic, strong, vigorous, determined not to put up with any crap. But they only lasted a few moments. What Siddhartha Mukherjee in *The Emperor of All Maladies* calls "the vulgarity of dying" frightened her more than death itself. The future was terrifying, the present was becoming unbearable at a quickening rate. The stairs were almost beyond her strength and balance now, she needed to be spoon-fed, she could no longer hold her toothbrush. Walking from the front door to the tack room, a journey of about a hundred feet, was no longer possible even with help and the use of a walker; Miguel and the barn crew brushed away snow, cleared away ice, put down sand daily, preparing the way for Margaret with such care and devotion that they might have been responding to Isaiah's call "to make straight the high-way," but the distance was too much for her. She was increasingly housebound, a sad fate for someone whose lifelong passion it was to be outdoors in every daylight hour.

About a week after her latest visit to Alain she fell again, this time on her way back to bed after getting up to go to the bath-room, even though I was holding on to her. She landed on the floor beside the bed. I was not strong enough to lift her up and put her back on the bed, she had no strength in her legs to help me, so eventually I had to call Miguel and Maria to come over in the middle of the night, and after she had been made decent by Maria—Margaret's nightgown had bunched up around her shoulders—Miguel and I lifted her off the floor and put her into bed. Although her speech was by now indistinct and difficult to understand she made a great effort to say slowly, enunciating each word as clearly as she could, "Enough, we can't do this anymore."

It was clear to me that the next step was hospice care at home. *Palliative care*, which Alain had suggested in his letter to Dr. Rubin, would involve caring for her in an outpatient setting or a hospital without attempting to treat the systemic disease; *hospice care*, which was also called *end-of-life care*, would involve keeping her as comfortable and as pain-free as possible without attempting to impede or slow down the inevitable, and was for patients with a life expectancy of six months or less.

Hospice care is an old idea, dating back to the eleventh century, when hospices were founded by religious orders, initially to care for the sick, the wounded, and the incurably ill as they returned from the Crusades. Since in those days almost everybody who sought such help died, the word *hospice* eventually came to signify a place in which to die, as opposed to a *hospital*, which signified a place in which one hoped to be healed. With the decline of the religious orders, hospices too drifted out of use in the English-speaking world until revived on a large scale in the twentieth century, stripped by this time of a religious identity.

In the eighteenth and the nineteenth centuries it became more usual to die at home, if possible surrounded by family. Indeed, "the deathbed scene" became a staple of fiction, and the obligatory last chapter in any biography. Deathbed scenes, moving or horrifying, dot the works of almost every English novelist, Dickens being the most memorable—little Nell's death in *The Old Curiosity Shop* is the most famous in English literature. Doctors mostly played no major role at the deathbed except to sit help-lessly by the bedside, gold pocket watch in hand, feeling the pulse of the dying patient to pronounce the death when it happened.

After the First World War it became more frequent (and was considered more "modern") for people to die in a hospital, with consequences with which we remain familiar—patients dying while wired up to monitors and kept breathing with tubes in the throat or the nose, attached to a ventilator and IV drips. It is, after all, the purpose of hospitals, doctors, and nurses to keep patients *alive*, not to let them die.

It was with this in mind that Dame Cicely Saunders founded St. Christopher's Hospice in London in 1967, and set in motion a movement that has since spread throughout the English-speaking world to focus on the "total pain" of a dying patient, that is, both the physical pain and the anxiety, and to provide comfort for the patient rather than attempting to prolong life.

Even for those who are very ill—and for those who love them—seeking hospice care is a difficult decision. I could not help feeling guilty for abandoning hope, illusions, faith in miracles or an improbable last-minute reprieve as I made the decision to seek home hospice care for Margaret. For those patients in unremit-ting pain it is perhaps an easier decision, but Margaret was not in physical pain, she was in a state of intense anxiety at the prospect of encroaching helplessness and death.

As I was soon to discover, anxiety is every bit as terrible as pain, and perhaps its equal. Pain can be controlled by medica-tions up to a point, even at the risk of placing the patient in a state of suspended animation, but so long as the patient's *mind* is working there is no way to stop him or her from thinking, *I am dying, I will soon be dead*, no combination of drugs and pain-killers can prevent the patient from knowing what is going to happen in weeks, days, hours, or minutes. Hardly anything could be more anxiety-producing than that. The shelves at CVS are full of "get well" cards, funny or sentimental, to send to those who are ill, but there are none for those in hospice care that read, "Die well," or even more unlikely, "Die soon." We do not deal easily with the fact that somebody we know or love is facing death, and *knows* it; still less with the idea that death, which we spend our lives denying, putting off, or struggling against, is now the best outcome. Every step I made toward putting Margaret into home hospice care felt as if I were condemning her to death, and yet I knew it had to be done. I would just have to live with my guilt feelings, I decided.

Colleen had already connected me to Hudson Valley Hospice, and getting Margaret enrolled there did not present any problems. Despite the dogged cheerfulness of the HVH staff, there was no way to soften the reality. Margaret would have an HVH "case manager," Donna Engle, who would visit her as soon as possible. HVH would deliver a fully adjustable hospital bed with sheets and pillows, a bedside commode, an adjustable hospital "over-bed table," a wheelchair, oxygen, briefs, pads, and other continence-care supplies, gloves, adult wet wipes, a bedpan, and much else besides. I said that I wasn't sure about the hospital bed, Margaret's strongest wish was to die in her own bed, I thought the sight of a hospital bed might alarm her, but we compromised by agreeing to put it between the cars in the garage until it was needed. A truck would bring these supplies, with two people to carry everything and put it all in place. Sifting through the paperwork, I saw it included a small printed brochure entitled *When Death Is Near: A Caregiver's Guide* and a typed four-page list describing "Signs of Approaching Death." I put these to one side and out of sight to read later, with considerable foreboding.

There is a certain relief, at any rate for the caregiver, in putting the patient in the hands of home hospice care. First of all, there is backup, someone to go to day or night with a problem or a question; second, there's organization and support, a framework in which to care for the patient. I remembered the famous line from Graham Greene's screenplay for *The Third Man,* "Death's at the bottom of everything . . . leave death to the professionals." It was a film Margaret and I had often watched together, sitting downstairs in the library, or upstairs stretched out on the bed, with a couple of Margaret's cats lying between us or curled at her feet. Most eighteenth century houses have small bedrooms—it was hard to keep them warm back then—but by some fluke ours was huge, and over the years Margaret had got it exactly the way she wanted it, with a chaise longue over in one corner (which she never used), big comfortable chairs, souvenirs and knickknacks from her travels spread out everywhere. She liked to lie there on winter afternoons, after riding and walking in the morning, to do the *Times* crossword puzzle (in ink, of course) in the company of her cats. As I explained to Donna, a warm, smart, patient, and experienced nurse, this was where she wanted to die, not in a hospital bed. Donna did not seem surprised, she had no doubt dealt with far stranger requests during her career. Her practiced eye took in trouble spots, small rugs that could easily lead to a fall, not to speak of the highly polished eighteenth century wide-plank pine floor, which was only too easy to slip on even for someone in good health, places where if Margaret fell she might hit her head against a sharp corner. There would have to be a certain amount of shuffling around of furniture in the interest of safety, convenience, and comfort.

I anticipated some degree of resistance or shock from Margaret; transitioning to home hospice care is in effect making death certain, it's generally limited to patients who have less than six months to live, and in fact many people (or their families) don't choose hospice care until shortly before death. That Margaret knew she was dying was one thing—of course she did by then—but becoming a hospice care patient set the official seal on the fact. Her oncologist, Dr. Rubin had certified it, Medicare had signed off on it (Medicare A covers hospice care 100 percent), HVH had accepted her as patient, she was now *officially* dying, it was no longer a faraway event or one about which there could be any doubt. Although Margaret would hardly have been aware of it, medical decisions would now be made by her hospice team; her doctors might be consulted, but day-to-day care would be in the hands of HVH henceforth, with the aim of making her comfortable rather than "curing" her. She showed no surprise when Colleen sat down beside the bed and broke the news to her. If anything she seemed relieved to be in good hands. Margaret's decreasing mobility and growing helplessness—there was now almost nothing she could do for herself—made it clear to her that she needed professional help, much as she didn't want to be surrounded by strangers or subjected to anything resembling a hospital routine.

When Colleen had gone I sat down beside Margaret. "It's good that we'll have the home hospice care started soon," I said, holding her hand. It felt tiny and cold.

"I don't want anything changed."

I looked around. Nothing much *had* been changed so far, except that the big oak table on which the television set sat was cluttered with boxes of first-aid dressings and everything needed to care for the wounds on Margaret's legs. The bedroom looked just as it had when Thom von Bulow had redecorated the house a few years ago, paid for by an unexpected (and regrettably brief) surge of movie option money; it had looked a bit shabby before, and now it had a certain English chic-shabbiness. Margaret possessed to a degree that surprised most people all of the domestic skills: she could decorate a house, iron a shirt, pleat a skirt, cook a crown roast of lamb for a dozen people, polish silver until it shone like a mirror. At some point in her life she had picked up all that from her mother Kit, whose standards in such matters were those of Edwardian England, not to speak of Margaret's father

Paul, who would briskly reject an overcooked vegetable or a glass with a fingerprint on it. Until equine competition took over her life, Margaret loved decorating—upholstery fabrics, pillows, curtains, every pillow and piece of furniture in the bedroom meant something to her.

"We'll change as little as possible," I said, wondering where we were going to put the commode, or if it could be hidden for a while. But that would surely defeat its purpose?

Margaret lay propped up on pillows, hardly moving. It was difficult to remember that only a few weeks ago she had been riding, walking, driving, planning to go down to the city and visit the wig shop with Tom. Since April of last year our lives had been dominated by what Margaret's next MRI would show, but quite suddenly it no longer mattered—another MRI would merely show us what we already knew, that she was dying, and that she would probably not live long enough to try on the wig that Tom was having made for her.

"I just wish it were over," she said.

I had not been expecting a call from our nearest neighbor Thom Schwartz, a tall, slim, grave, neatly bearded man who resembled Saint Francis of Assisi without the tonsure or the robe, or at any rate the stone statue of him that stood in our garden close to the birdbath. Thom was Margaret's favorite neighbor—he did not shoot deer out of season on our land, or ride a four-wheeler or a snowmobile on it, or set traps; occasionally he and his children walked on it, but he always asked permission before doing so, and on the rare occasions when we met him he was always charming, considerate, and softly spoken. He had a sharp sense of humor that matched Margaret's. I had known that Thom and his wife were both nurses, but until he came by and talked to me about

Margaret I had not realized that he was one of the night nurses on call at Hudson Valley Hospice, very likely the person I would soon be reaching out to whenever something went wrong at night. We exchanged cell phone numbers, and chatted about how to look after Margaret. I said that so far I didn't think I had done all that well. I had probably done better than I supposed, he said. Most people thought they had failed some kind of test, but there wasn't one. He too thought that 24/7 care would be a good idea, but I would know when it was time for that when I got there. I should call him whenever I had a problem, day or night. "This, *this*, is the hardest and best thing you'll ever do," he would write later, and that is pretty much what he told me then.

He was right.

As the world narrowed down for Margaret, it inevitably narrowed down for me as well. Looking after someone who is dying gradually fills one's life to the exclusion of everything else, it's on-the-job training to the nth degree, there's no manual that tells you what to do, what to expect, what to tell the person who's dying. I had managed to find an agency that supplied around-the-clock nurses, which I could already tell we were going to need. This turned out to be a time-consuming and aggravating challenge, unlike enrolling Margaret in home hospice care, and was not covered by Medicare. The agency would provide two nurses a day, one from eight a.m. to eight p.m., the other to cover the night shift, and we labored mightily to deal with the paperwork and to draw up a schedule—it was obvious to me that until I got to know the nurses a lot of my time would be spent managing this, explaining how to find us in the boonies, and making sure that people arrived on time to replace each other.

Dawn and I set up a cork bulletin board on an easel in my

office, with each day divided in two so we could plot who was coming when, keep track of the names, and record their cell phone numbers. It occurred to me that my solution to the emotional challenge of looking after Margaret was to keep busy, but that did not mean it was make-work, it still all needed to be done. Planning is an affirmation of life; looking back on it, I realize that I was drawing up charts of day and night care extending far beyond the amount of time Margaret had left to live—it was a way of ignoring reality, perhaps of even supposing that one could prevent it, like someone drawing up a mental shopping list as their car skids toward an accident: "I *will* live, I *will* buy ketchup, paper towels, toilet paper, cat food . . ." Anchoring the mind in the humdrum routines of life has a calming effect because it suggests that at least *something* is under control. One can't halt the progress of the disease, or even slow it down, but one can make plans, lists, buy supplies, make sure the patient is comfortable. As if keeping busy were a solution to something, I became the master of the checklist.

It is a measure of Margaret's increasing isolation—unable to talk except with extreme difficulty, unable to email, increasingly unable to walk, to pick up a spoon, to wipe herself, to brush her teeth—that I managed to get the stair lift people to install it in one day without her even noticing that it was going on, although it was all taking place within a few feet from her. It came as promised, prefabricated pieces that clipped into place without a problem, and I caught a break toward the end of the day to take an inaugural test ride on it, feeling slightly foolish as I went silently down and back up the stairs, with my seat belt fastened—here was at least one useful improvement accomplished.

One of the reasons I had for getting it installed in the first place was to take Margaret out to the barn to see her horses, which I thought might cheer her up a bit. I explained it all to her at teatime in the bedroom: the stair lift would take her smoothly downstairs, I had tried it myself, we could wheel her across the dining room to the front porch, then carry the wheelchair outside, push her to the barn to see her horses, and bring her back upstairs again without a problem. I had imagined it as a cheerful scene, Margaret wrapped up in her warm coat with a blanket over her legs, feeding her horses a treat, with myself and the barn guys smiling in the background. I may have sounded a touch overenthusiastic about it, as if I were selling her something, because she listened quietly, then shook her head. "No," she said.

We didn't have to do it today, I assured her, it was getting late and dark anyway, we could do it tomorrow or the next day, it would be easier in the daylight.

"No," she repeated, and her expression told me everything I needed to know.

She had already said goodbye to all that, without drama, the last time she was in the barn.

The stair lift never got used.

14.

IT SHOULD COME as no surprise that caring for the dying brings one back to the basics of living, not just in the sense of looking after the bodily needs of the dying person, which inevitably become closer day by day to those of an infant, but to the *spiritual* needs, which increasingly involves presence, and touch. To talk to the person who is dying, even if he or she can no longer reply, signifies one's presence; to touch, to hold hands, to hug the person who is dying is to be for a moment at one with them.

The Hindu spiritual leader and guru Mata Amritanandamayi (Amma) has based her entire message on this, having apparently hugged millions of people over thirty years. Amma is not necessarily a saint as we define sainthood in Western terms, she does not for example perform miracles, nor does she convey a blessing in the sense that a priest might. People tell her their troubles, she listens patiently, then she wipes their tears and hugs them. A huge international order has grown around her from this simple beginning, some of it devoted to such ambitious social schemes as cleaning India's rivers, disposing of its overwhelming garbage, or building toilets—as always in India, it is difficult to separate the secular from the religious impulse—but at its core is the simple act of hugging a stranger.

Or a loved one. It was Alain, a neurosurgeon attuned to *dar-shana*, who brought Amma to my attention, when he emailed me on March 28 about the results of Margaret's CT scan. "[Amma] exudes love and compassion for all by simply touching and holding people against her," he wrote. "We are all in need of love and in this trying moment for you and Margaret I hold the two of you in my thoughts . . . The fact that a CT scan showed additional tumors in the lungs comes as no surprise. Obviously the cancer has spread unchecked throughout her body . . . At this point my feeling is that enough has been done in terms of medical interventions. She has been very brave but there comes a time when we have to accept that all life must pass."

⌣

"*. . . all life must pass.*" I read this message again and again, touched and impressed by its compassion and wisdom. It confirmed what I had come to believe many weeks ago, that what mattered most now was to make Margaret as comfortable as I could physically, and to be present for her as much as possible, for surely the worst thing about dying is the terrible sense of loneliness, the knowledge that you are going, quickly or slowly, with or without pain, to where you can no longer be reached, ever, and going there alone. More than anything it is the *loneliness* of dying that frightens those approaching death as much as death itself.

The world had closed in tightly around Margaret, first confining her to the house, then to her bedroom, finally to her bed. Day by day the bedroom began to resemble a hospital room as the supplies and the equipment from Hudson Valley Hospice slowly but inexorably began to take over every surface. The wheelchair, folded now, the walker and the canes, were pushed out of the way into a corner of the room, a sign that Margaret was not going to be needing them anymore, that it was bedsores we would be worrying about soon, not her slipping on the floor or tripping on a rug.

It was clear to me that I would need to start 24/7 nursing care shortly. I didn't think Margaret would like the idea, each step in extending her care must have seemed to her as if she were losing control over every part of her life, being reduced to an object that was being looked after rather than a person, but practically speaking I couldn't see any way to get her through a night safely at this point without help. I felt guilty about making decisions Margaret would have wanted to make by herself, or at least be involved in, but there was no longer a choice.

I consoled myself with the fact that we had three guest bedrooms, so I could put the nurse in one of them and fetch her when she was needed, Margaret would not have to see her except when it was necessary. I didn't have to worry about whether the guest bedrooms were ready; they were always ready, with a new bar of soap in the bathroom, a fresh box of Kleenex, an intercom system on the telephone, miniature bottles of shampoo and body lotion, plenty of towels, all the comforts of a good hotel room— Margaret wasn't her mother's daughter for nothing. As it happened, we had not had any guests since her illness began, but we were always ready for them.

It was not just guests that Margaret didn't want, she also didn't want visitors. I had suggested to her that if she wanted to see her goddaughter Tamzin, now was the time to do it. I had emailed Tamzin to tell her how things stood, that Margaret was in hospice care, that she was more or less confined to her bed, and that no further treatment was planned or possible, and Tamzin had offered to fly from the UK at once. Ordinarily, Margaret would have been overjoyed to see Tamzin, but she shook her head and even was able to say, "No!" vigorously.

I was surprised, and even disappointed. Of all people, Tamzin was the best at organizing things, and, speaking selfishly, her company would have pleased me, but I should have known better. Years before, when Margaret heard from Tamzin's mother that her father Paul Mogford was dying at a local "cottage hospital" near the village of Broadway in England where Margaret had grown up, we decided we had better go and see him before it was too late.

In those days the supersonic British Airways Concorde was still flying, it was only three hours and fifteen minutes from JFK to Heathrow, so we took it, rented a car at Heathrow, and drove straight up to see Paul. When we entered his room he turned his back on us, he lay there silently, facing the wall of the tiny room he shared with another terminally ill patient. His back was partly exposed by the hospital gown—although Paul always had a trim figure, he had lost so much weight that each vertebra stood out separately, as if his spine had been prepared for an anatomy class. I thought that he might not want me, a comparative stranger, to see him like this, so I gave Margaret's hand a squeeze and stepped out of the room to leave them together.

A few minutes later she walked out, her face composed but white, her lips compressed.

"Did he say anything?" I asked. She shook her head.

"No, he wouldn't talk to me," she replied. "He wouldn't even *look* at me."

I suggested that we give him a little time, then try again— after all, we had flown across the Atlantic to see him, and we were not in a hurry—but Margaret said no, she knew her father, he wouldn't change his mind, and that was that.

"Let's just go home," she said firmly.

So we did just that. We drove back to Heathrow, returned the car, took the next westbound Concorde, and were back in New York City on the same day we had left it. I thought then that it was vanity on Paul's part—he was the most fastidious of men, he managed the immense farm of the wealthy Holland-Martin family, always dressed in a perfectly pressed tweed suit and gleaming shoes, a striking, handsome figure of a man. But I came to realize that it was more than this—he was a man who kept a tight control of everything, himself included, he hadn't asked Margaret to fly over and see him dying, from his point of view we had forced ourselves on him, and he neither approved of our visit, nor did he want Margaret to see him helpless. We had violated his privacy. Had she asked Paul first if he would like her to visit him, he would probably have said with gruff affection, *Don't waste your money, girl.*

He died two days later, and when we flew over again it was to dispose of his ashes, and Kit's, for she died in a separate nursing home of the complications of senile dementia. Paul had placed her there, and never once went back to visit her, she would no longer have recognized him anyway, and he was not one for useless sentimental gestures. In the end Tamzin's father and I scattered Kit and Paul's ashes in the duck pond behind where they had lived for nearly fifty years. I felt an inexpressible sadness for the death of two people I had hardly known as Mike Blinkhorn and I gathered up the empty containers for the ashes, which looked very much like vacuum flasks.

People supposed that Margaret didn't want her friends and those she loved to see her as she was now out of vanity, and of course that may have been partly true, but what mattered most to her was that like her father she didn't want to be seen helpless, above all she didn't need or want pity. Lying in bed with her hands trembling, unable to brush her own teeth or blow her own nose, was not the way she wanted Tamzin, or anyone else, to remember her. She wouldn't see her friend Linda, like her slim, blond, and athletic, who drove up from Ridgefield, Connecticut, three or four times a week to exercise Margaret's horses. She told me to say no to all the friends who wanted to see her. The only exceptions she made were for Megan, who was something like a surrogate daughter and could tell Margaret how her horses were doing; Megan's mother Colleen, who was an LPN, and therefore had professional standing and could deal with Margaret's wounds and with the best way of keeping her comfortable; of course Laura, and the HVH nurses who came in once a day to make sure she was being properly looked after—they too were professionals. Dawn, as well, could come upstairs and visit her—now that Margaret was unable to deal with phone calls or reply to emails, Dawn was the person she trusted to fend off friends who wanted to see her, or at least speak to her.

⁓⌒

I called the nurse care provider and told her that we needed to get started, and we agreed to begin that night at eight o'clock. What did I need to provide for the nurse? I asked. Nothing, she replied, he would bring his own food, fruit juice, and water. "He?" For some reason I had always assumed that the nurses would be women, which had been the case up to now. It turned out that "he" was Sylvan Wilson, and that he was Jamaican. I contemplated this with a certain doubt. I wasn't sure how Margaret would feel about being cared for by a man. I didn't think the fact that Sylvan was Jamaican would matter, Margaret was not a bigot, but I would have preferred to start 24/7 care with someone with whom Margaret might bond more easily, like Laura, with whom she had bonded instantly. "Sylvan is the best we've got," the nurse care manager said, "you'll see." I wished there had been a chance to audition the prospective nurses, but that had not been possible, and it was in any case too late now.

I told Margaret that a night nurse was coming, which she

accepted with something between resignation and relief; at least there would be no more accidents. I fed her dinner—I was still bringing in food, this time Japanese food from the Tokyo Tavern in Pleasant Valley, she was quite fond of their avocado rolls and the hibachi shrimp. I chopped everything up until it was virtually puréed, and fed it to her by spoon, alternating each spoonful with a sip of water through a straw, and reinforced it with a bottle of chocolate or vanilla Ensure. The main thing was to do everything very slowly. She ate very little, but the meals at least gave some shape to her day, and she quite liked to see the food neatly laid out on a tray, with a vodka tonic beside the plate—even though she did not eat much of it or take more than a sip of her vodka tonic, the sight of it all cheered her up a bit. Spoon-feeding her was a trial for both of us. I was terrified she would choke, and after even a few spoonfuls she had eaten as much as she wanted—she looked forward to dinner but she hated the fact that it was followed by the tedious routine of brushing her teeth and getting her ready for the night. On the other hand, Margaret was fanatic about caring for teeth, even in the most difficult of circumstances. On safari, for example, she flossed and brushed meticulously three times a day, which is perhaps why unlike most people in England she had perfect teeth despite all that sugar and chocolate. It might have been thought that taking care of her teeth would be the least of Margaret's concerns now that she was dying, but this was not so. It had to be done for her by one of the nurses, using a stainless steel emesis basin, it mattered as much to her as ever.

The nights seemed endlessly long and difficult, Margaret slept badly despite the sleeping pills, and the only thing that soothed her was the presence of one of her cats on the bed. Kit Kat, normally quick to scratch, was snuggled at Margaret's feet or curled up beside her, as was Ruby, a kind of feline Florence Nightingale who had nursed Mr. McT, an oversized bully of a cat, when he was dying of cancer, embracing him with her front paws. I do not like to anthropomorphize cats, or any other animal, but the cats both knew Margaret was ill, they may even have known she was dying, and took shifts on the bed, changing place at two-hour intervals without any fuss so she was never alone. Kit Kat was usually aggressive with strangers, while Ruby normally hid when anyone she didn't know came upstairs, but both cats overcame their natural instincts to stay as close to Margaret as they could get, purring away so she knew they were there. Her hands shook too violently to make stroking them easy.

I took the tray downstairs and cleaned up, and promptly at eight the doorbell rang. Sylvan was tall, broad-shouldered, dressed in white athletic clothes, a down jacket, and a jaunty cowboy hat, and hugely cheerful. The combination of a West Indian accent and my deafness made it hard for me to understand him at first, but it was clear at once that he was overwhelmingly friendly and competent. He was carrying several plastic bags, which he put in the refrigerator—his dinner, he explained. I began to tell him about the guest rooms and the intercom, but he laughed. It was his job to be close to the patient, not to sleep, I needn't worry about him, he would make himself comfortable. I thought I should probably introduce him to Margaret, but he politely waved the suggestion away—it would be better if he went up and introduced himself to her. That seemed to me unlikely, but as I was soon to discover Sylvan was a force of nature, hard to deflect. He bounded upstairs carrying his coat and a bottle of water. I waited anxiously at the foot of the stairs in case she protested, but I heard nothing except subdued murmurs. I gave them half an hour, then went up to see how things were going.

Sylvan had pulled a chair close to Margaret and was talking to her in a deep, gentle voice. Clearly, they were bonding. She seemed relaxed, and even the trembling of her hands was less severe. Contrary to my fears, Sylvan rapidly became one of her favorite nurses, so much so that when he arrived one night without his usual bag full of food for himself she made sure that I drove to Ray's deli to get Sylvan his dinner. She asked every afternoon if Sylvan was coming, and when told that he was, she visibly relaxed.

What was most striking to me was just how good most of the nurses were; the fact that Margaret was dying did not change their attitude toward her, they were almost universally attentive, caring, and gentle, even though they were not specialists in hospice care like the nurses from HVH. In their hands Margaret was always made as comfortable as she could be, there was never the slightest hint of the indifference to the patient about which so many people complain. These nurses *cared.* And the people from HVH were beyond praise, whether it was Donna; Margaret's nurse case manager, Priscilla, who came every two days to give Margaret a sponge bath; Marialice, who came by frequently to check her vital signs; or Thom, who took the time on his way to work or on his way home to drop in, kneel down by Margaret's bed, and talk to her.

All the same, Margaret's decline was increasing. From time to time she was able to speak, but it was often impossible to understand what she was trying to say. Sylvan and Laura were able to get her out of bed to use the commode for a few days, but on March 30 Donna decided it was time to put in a catheter. That too was a setback, a further increase of her helplessness, confirmation that Margaret would never get out of this bed. She was as firmly trapped as an animal in a snare, there was no relief, and no escape.

When we first bought our house in Dutchess County nearly four decades ago we had no idea about the number of people who had been given permission over the years to use the land by the previous owners: the local fox hunt, deer hunters, bird shooters (pheas-ant, geese, wild turkey, duck), snowmobilers, bird-watchers, to name but a few. We tried to deal fairly with all these people and more, compromising on those Margaret could live with—bird-watchers, for example, or fox hunters—and saying no to those she couldn't, like deer hunters. After all, you don't want to live in a state of constant vendetta with your neighbors. But it came as a surprise to us during our first winter to find a raccoon with one foot caught in an animal trap. It had tried to chew its foot off to get free but failed, and was lying in a pool of its own blood on the snow staring at us. This was in the age before cell phones, so I cantered back to the barn and asked Richard Bacon, the husband of Roxy Bacon, who looked after our horses, to get his .22 and put the raccoon out of its misery, which he did. I told the fur trapper the next day that we didn't want him setting snares or traps on the land anymore—it had never occurred to either of us that there *was* anyone still fur-trapping only ninety miles from New York City— but I have never forgotten the look in that raccoon's eyes, not fear or anger, it was past all that, just deep, bottomless despair.

I saw the same look in Margaret's eyes now, as I sat holding her hand and talking to her. Talking to someone who is dying is never easy. Dwelling on happy times in the past risks making them feel worse rather than better, knowing that they are leaving all that behind; talking about the future is pointless when there is none. The words one must *never* say are, *You're going to get better, you'll see*, which is what we all instinctively want to say to those who are sick, even *very* sick—optimism is the best thing we have to offer, even when we don't believe it ourselves, for it is often true that if people *think* they are going to get better, they might. Hope is a wonder drug, as every doctor knows, the oldest one, and it sometimes performs miracle cures. But it is a pointless cruelty to preach optimism to someone who is dying and knows it. Margaret knew she was dying, she would have known it anyway—you don't go into hospice care without know-ing what the end will be. I found it best to acknowledge that and talk about how her horses would be looked after, and her cats, and explain what I intended to do with them, practical matters like that. When she did not agree, she shook her head; when she agreed, she nodded. She was not in pain, whenever she was asked that she shook her head, she was on a heavy dose of haloperidol (Haldol) and lorazepam (Ativan) every four hours, which kept her composed. At this point she was hardly able to eat anything, she was drinking Ensure through a straw. As I emailed a friend, "Speech almost impossible, also use of hands, everything shut-ting down, kidneys, etc., melanoma tumors in both lungs, terrible to watch."

I had been sleeping beside Margaret, but this was no longer practical since a nurse was beside her all the time, not to speak of one of the cats, so I had a folding cot set up outside in the hallway by the bedroom door—that way the nurse could call me if there was a problem but I would not be in the way. As long as I was within hearing next to the bedroom door, Margaret was satisfied, but it made her nervous if I went downstairs or left the house.

It came to me as I sat and held her hand that what this was now was the deathwatch.

15.

THE BODILY FUNCTIONS don't stop at once. The catheter needs to be kept clean, the catheter bag has to be emptied regularly, bowel movements require shifting the patient and careful cleaning afterward, lotion needs to be rubbed into the skin. By the first week of April Margaret could do nothing for herself, keeping her clean and comfortable was day and night a full-time job. It meant too that we seldom had much time with just the two of us together—with 24/7 care there was nearly always something going on in the bedroom, if only in the background. One night, when Sylvan was on his break downstairs eating his supper in the kitchen, Margaret did her best to squeeze my hand, and, trying hard to articulate each word, said, after several tries, "Let me go," with a long pause between each word.

I understood exactly what she meant, she was talking about euthanasia—an early interest of my son Chris's, who attained a certain notoriety early on in his life by founding a pro-euthanasia group that was somewhere between a cult and an activist collective, and produced a degree of outrage that is still reverberating three decades later. I was not *against* euthanasia in principle—had it been legal in New York State I might even have been in favor of it for someone in Margaret's condition—but I had a strong reluctance to being her killer, which is what it amounted to. During the year since her diagnosis Margaret had never shown any sign of being suicidal, even when faced with news that might have made anyone consider it. She kept a treasure trove of sleeping pills, pain medications, even laudanum (tincture of opium, an old-fashioned but effective remedy for diarrhea) in a flowered zipper bag in her closet, just in case she ran out of her supply of sleeping pills or was suffering from pain or a bad cold or stomach trouble when she was competing, but she was not an addict, she never exceeded the prescribed dose that she took every day. The zipper bag was insurance; as long as she knew it was there (or in her baggage) she wasn't worried.

Between what was in my bathroom medicine cabinet and hers, not to speak of her "stash" in the closet, there was enough in the house to commit suicide many times over, and that is without taking into account that she had a carry pistol permit and owned two pistols, one of them always kept loaded in the drawer of the bedside table on her side of the bed (a legacy of her time in Kenya during the Mau-Mau "troubles") and her over-and-under twenty-gauge shotgun propped against the bedroom mantelpiece. I did not take any of this away from her, or even unload her pistol— to do so would have shown a lack of confidence in her that she would have deeply resented, besides, in my experience people who want to commit suicide will always find a way to do it. One of our neighbors did so by injecting herself with a syringe full of horse tranquilizer from the medicine cabinet of her barn. Margaret's closest friend Robin had committed suicide in 2011 at the age of fifty-seven when he reached the end of his tether. Robin called her the night he did it to say goodbye, and she tried to talk him out of it. She understood why he had decided to die, but she thought he was being cruel to those who loved him; her own instinct was always to carry on in the face of difficulty. She felt the same about the suicide of another friend, who killed himself with an overdose of alcohol and sleeping pills, after taking which he wrapped a plastic bag around his head to suffocate himself. Margaret thought his suicide was his final bid for attention, and his method of doing it was gruesome. In any case, if suicide had ever seriously tempted her during her illness it was now too late, that ship had sailed, she could no longer do it herself.

The thought of doing it *for* her had of course occurred to me, that was only natural in the circumstances; had she been an animal I would not have hesitated, but she was not. There were practical difficulties too. I had no idea what a lethal dose of lorazepam or clonazepam might be, but I *did* know that getting it wrong might result in Margaret surviving in hospital for some time with severe brain damage in a vegetative state like Claus von Bulow's wife Sunny, hardly an outcome Margaret would want, and I had a natural reluctance to call my son Chris and ask him how much of either medication I had to give his stepmother to kill her. Furthermore, now that a caregiver was present day and night it would be impossible to give Margaret a whole lot of pills without being noticed; each one had to be placed on a wood tongue depressor, followed by giving her a small amount of liquid through a straw and making sure she swallowed it. It was a slow process even for a single small pill, let alone a fatal dose of pills one by one.

Then too there was the moral-ethical question, quite apart from the practical and the legal ones—killing someone you love is a different matter than putting an ailing pet down or a trapped raccoon. Margaret and I both held each other's health care proxy and DNR, but not resuscitating a patient in cardiac arrest is a world away from killing him or her. In a large family there might have been a chance to sit down and discuss it, although who knows how many families actually do so, but there were, in effect, just the two of us, I was on my own. I took her hand—the trembling was acute now—and said, "I'll see what I can do, but I can't do that."

Margaret did not seem surprised, she nodded and closed her eyes. Was that a sign that she accepted my decision, or that she had anticipated it? I made a mental note to find out if her medication could be increased, not to the point of killing her, but to the point of altogether dulling her anxiety. As a start, I doubled the dose of her sleeping pills—we had enough of them, so that wouldn't be difficult, nor was it likely to set off any alarm bells among the caregivers. Once she was asleep and Sylvan was back from his dinner I lay down on my cot outside the door—Margaret was calm as long as I was within hearing—and opened the HVH pamphlet on what to do when death is near. Before, I had glanced at it superficially, thinking there was still plenty of time for that, but I decided I had better read it carefully now.

The exhortation on the front page to "let the pure light within you guide you on your way" I dismissed—it was a nice thought, but like much of the language surrounding death it assumed a degree of spirituality or faith that I did not think Margaret possessed any more than I did. Serenity was not her strong point, and I did not think she was at present searching for "the pure light," although if it existed I hoped she would find it. The second page was less touchy-feely, a straightforward comment on the importance of providing comfort and support to someone entering this last phase of life, but the table of contents got down to the nitty-gritty: "Changes in Elimination," "Restlessness and Agitation," "Surge of Energy," and "Moment of Death."

I resisted reading the end first, which is what I usually do with how-to material, since the last chapter or paragraph very often sums up everything before it, and I began at the beginning. It was reassuring to know that withdrawal from friends, family, and the world is a normal part of the dying process. That was certainly true for Margaret, and there was a certain comfort to knowing that she wasn't alone, that this was a normal part of dying. "Changes in Appetite," that was certainly happening—

Margaret was no longer tempted by any of the things she normally enjoyed. "Changes in Elimination" were taking place, it had been necessary to add a glass of warm prune juice to her diet, and we had already inserted a catheter. "Changes in Breathing" had not yet occurred, nor extreme variations in body temperature. So far there was no sign of confusion and disorientation; on the contrary Margaret's mind seemed as sharp as ever, she was simply losing her ability to express herself as a result of the tumor's increasing "mass effect," or pressure, on the left side of her brain. I did not think that "reading something inspirational or playing soft music" would calm Margaret's anxiety; there had been a harpist playing at times in the lobby of the Wellness and Cancer Center at Northern Westchester Hospital, but the music got on Margaret's nerves rather than soothing her.

I thought that playing Willie Nelson singing "Always on My Mind" might be more likely to soothe Margaret, as well as *The Phantom of the Opera* and the sound track from the 1993 movie *Gettysburg*. None of these were necessarily inspirational, but Margaret played them so often that from time to time I had to replace the CDs in her car. "Surge of Energy" had not yet taken place, nor "Saying Goodbye," which would obviously be the most difficult moment, and for which HVH recommended, "Listen to the wisdom of your heart, and follow its guidance," which did not sound any more helpful than letting the pure light guide Margaret. The last chapter was "Care for the Caregiver," which consisted of solid commonsensical advice, much of which, I realized, I had not been following. I had not been going outside at regular intervals to smell and feel the fresh air, despite the first signs of beautiful spring weather, or doing deep breathing exercises, or lying down for twenty minutes at a time, or drinking plenty of water—in fact, I was drinking more bourbon than usual, and starting in on it earlier, which was probably not a good idea. I had not given much thought to the need to stay fit and alert throughout Margaret's passage toward death, however long that might be. Caring for her would obviously demand a degree of physical stamina from me, as well as a firm emotional balance. "It is the hardest thing you will ever do," Thom had warned me, and who would know better?

He was right too. Putting the dying person in the best possible hospice is one thing—family, loved ones can visit him or her every day, depending on the visiting hours—but *home* hospice care puts you face-to-face with the dying person twenty-four hours a day, there is no driving home when visiting hours are over to have a drink, a bath, warm up dinner, look at the mail, then go back to the hospice again the next day. Of course, I was fortunate Margaret had 24/7 care, which makes a huge difference, but even allowing for that I was still the backup for things that require more than one person, like lifting Margaret in bed and cleaning her up after a bowel movement—it's as if life had been suddenly taken over by piles of disposable adult wipes and StayDry underpads. Big plastic tubs that had to be emptied twice a day replaced the wastepaper baskets, Aloe Vesta ointment had to be massaged into Margaret's skin in the hope of preventing bedsores, Q-tips had to be used to clean up secretions from her eyes, foam rubber oral mouth swabs replaced a regular toothbrush, a mass of medical supplies began to fill the bedroom. Thom would eloquently write of it, "Dying is often—in my experience, usually—gruesome, excruciating, and hellishly long."

Margaret seemed to panic if I was out of sight for long, so I had an intercom put in that enabled the caregiver to call me if I had gone downstairs to my office or to the kitchen for a cup of tea, with a special buzzer for emergencies. I was never away for long, and seldom left the house at all, communicating with people mostly by email since I didn't want Margaret to overhear me answering questions about her condition. I emailed my son Chris to describe the situation: "Margaret is home, immobilized in bed . . . She is, frankly, dying, but no way to know how long it will take. She finds it difficult to speak due to brain surgeries, but wishes she were dead." To Alain, who had offered to drive up and visit her, I wrote: "Thanks for your generous offer, but Margaret finds it increasingly difficult to speak clearly, and I fear it might cause her additional stress . . . The problem is, frankly, *entre nous*, that she not only finds it difficult to speak, she is often incoherent, and her anxiety level and obsessive compulsive disorder are both terribly high . . . At the moment she doesn't want to see anybody, and flies into a panic if I leave her for only a few minutes. She is physically very strong but in the circumstances this is a mixed blessing. I think a visit would increase, rather than alleviate her mental problems."

～⌒

Margaret was like somebody drowning in the sea of her own anxiety, desperate for someone to throw her a life buoy, but there was no life buoy to throw. Donna advised increasing her Ativan dose, in the hope of giving her a little relief. When I held Margaret's hand it trembled uncontrollably and she gripped my fingers so hard that her nails dug into me, it was as if she were trying to hold on to life. The increased Ativan did help some, but it was still terrible for her, looking ahead to nothing. I found myself wishing she had some shred of religious belief to give her a sense of where she was going, of something after death—I wished it for myself too, but religious belief is not something you can develop at the last moment, and bringing in a pastor or a priest at this point, far from giving Margaret comfort, would only too likely be read by her merely as a sign of imminent death. "Long, difficult day," I wrote a friend, "it would be easier if her mind weren't sharp, but sadly while her speech is very muddled, it is."

The next day was worse still. "Margaret's level of anxiety is rising sky high," I wrote Alain, "and the hospice . . . has increased the dosage of Lorazepam to three 0.5MG sublingually a day, plus what she [gets] at night. They feel that the Dexamethasone (two a day) may be increasing her anxiety, and making her hyper, and wonders if it is still needed, or can be cut down at this point?" Alain agreed that it could be eliminated.

At this point, pills had to be slipped carefully under Margaret's tongue with a tongue depressor, she could no longer swallow them, and her mouth had to be kept closed until they dissolved under her tongue. The change in medication was made, and perhaps more important Donna added morphine every four hours to her other pills. The morphine worked miracles almost at once. For the next few days and nights Margaret's state of mind improved. I read several long emails aloud to her, one of them from Tamzin which she enjoyed, and she was able to take a little Activa yogurt every day and some Ensure. At times we were able to have something like a conversation, although it was hard for Margaret to find the right words and pronounce them. Still, she managed to say quite distinctly, "Field of Dreams," several times, with a look that clearly asked me to pay attention. I nodded and squeezed her hand, I understood her perfectly, she was talking about *her* "Field of Dreams," the name taken from the title of one of her favorite movies, starring Kevin Costner, in which the spirit of a dead baseball star tells the hero to plow under his corn and build a baseball diamond: "If you build it, he will come."

Margaret had taken seven acres of our land and turned them into a perfect cross-country riding course for herself, the grass as smooth as a cricket pitch, with seven of her favorite and most challenging jumps (or fences) arranged in a circle, including a hay wagon, a ditch, a table, and a big, solid log fence. When she was healthy, at the end of every ride she took her horse over the jumps, the last one a stone wall that Miguel had built for her, with a bush on either side. It was a test for horse and rider, they were all stiff jumps. Of course she would want to be buried there, it was her showpiece. I promised I would do it, and that seemed to calm her down. It was clearly something she had thought about carefully, and reached that decision, her mind was still working perfectly even as her body was failing.

A couple of days later she began to suffer from constipation, a result of the morphine. I emailed Donna to ask if we should give her two glasses of prune juice every day instead of one, I was worried that might bring on diarrhea, but she replied at once, "Give more prune juice, it is most healthy and has lots of fiber."

I could always count on a prompt reply full of firm commonsense from Donna, but by the next day Margaret took a turn for the worse. "Prune juice seems to have worked as you suggested," I reported, "however, Margaret is increasingly confused and incoherent, unable to finish sentences or find the right word, and constantly waving her hands about. Are these simply signposts along the way or are they likely to increase in severity?"

Margaret's hands moved all the time now, as if she were shadowboxing, but the movements were aimless and random, it was clearly not something she *willed*, it was automatic, out of her control, she was not even aware she was doing it, a sign of extreme agitation. At times she clawed at her skin or lips, tearing at her skin, drawing blood, and, more dangerous, tried to pluck at the tube of her catheter. I tried to hold her hands still, but that merely increased her agitation. This alarmed me, I wasn't sure the 24/7 caregivers could cope with it. Would they have to restrain her?

I reported this at once with alarm to Donna. "I am beginning to doubt the possibility of [continuing] to keep Margaret in home hospice care. Her acute mental distress, inability to speak clearly, and random picking at her skin and mouth that draws blood worry me very much."

Donna replied quickly, "It sounds like she is transitional," and instructed me to increase Margaret's dose of Haldol. "What means transitional?" I asked, and she emailed back, "Declining. Tom will explain. He is on the way."

Tom Herman was the HVH social worker, a man who was calm in any circumstances, indeed he positively *radiated* calm, which was just what I needed at the moment. He did not pretend to be a nurse, but he had the look of a man who had seen (or heard) everything when it came to dying. He thought I should talk to Donna about decreasing the interval between doses of Ativan, Haldol, and morphine, and not reach any hasty decision about moving Margaret to a hospice. If I decided to do it, he would make the necessary arrangements, but I should keep in mind that periods of hyperactivity would probably be followed by periods of exhaustion. Had I read the four typed pages I had received along with the pamphlet *When Death Is Near*? I had not. He gave me a look that suggested now was the time—even *past* the time—to read it. He would report back to Donna.

I left Margaret in Sylvan's care, went downstairs to my office, and found the four pages of *Signs of Approaching Death*. I had written "Oh, God!" on the first page after reading the title, and asked Dawn to file it away until I wanted it. Here it all was, reduced to the basics: "Appetite Changes," "Breathing," "Circulation" ("Some areas of the body, particularly around the lips, nail beds, and the part of the body on which the patient is lying become blue or purple in color."), "Confusion," "Dreams," "Eyes," "Fatigue," "Fever," "Loss of Body Functions," "Muscles," "Perspiration," "Restlessness," "Secretions." These signs of death would not necessarily appear in this exact order, but the definition of "Restlessness" described Margaret's condition exactly. "Occasionally, the patient may become restless. He/she may move around in bed, pull at the bed linens, or reach out and pick at the air." Under "Comfort Measures" for this condition, I read, "Do not try to stop the patient from picking at the air; it will only make him/her more agitated."

Picking at the air was disturbing to watch, it was like seeing someone who doesn't know how to swim desperately trying to save herself from drowning and failing. The look in Margaret's eyes was one of despair and terror, as if she were aware that she had lost control of her own body, the nervous system was detached from the thought process, it was merely a physical symptom of extreme agitation. Picking away at her own skin was worse. Was it a way of confirming that her body was still there, that she was still *alive*? I had known people in good health who did this until blood was running down their face, apparently unaware they were doing it. Was it a self-destructive impulse, or simply the need to feel *something*, even pain, and perhaps to inflict punishment on oneself, or to produce guilt in someone else? But for Margaret there was no conscious decision, she may not have even known she was doing it. As long as she did not try to pull out the catheter herself, which would be terrible, the worst she could do was make her skin bleed. The nurses tightened the bedcovers below her waist so she couldn't get her fingers around the catheter tube, tried to keep her hands from her face as much as possible, and took care of the skin injuries with antiseptic and Band-Aids.

We cut the interval between medications from once every four hours to once every three, with Valium added to the mix, and just as Thom had predicted Margaret lapsed into a precarious calm. Donna sent an LPN over to examine her and assess the situation. Margaret was now dozing, her hands were still, she was breathing regularly and apparently relaxed. "Margaret still sleeping," I emailed Thom that evening, "seemingly doesn't want to eat or drink anything, should I just let her sleep and give her sublingual Rx's at 8:30?" He emailed back that this was a good plan, and that he would stop by later or tomorrow. The next day Margaret seemed to rally a bit. "She is conscious and trying to communicate now," I emailed Donna in the morning, "but seems very weak, a rally, or part of the process?"

"Part of the process," she replied. You could always count on Donna to give you the straight truth.

Margaret struggled to speak, but she was not incoherent as she had been a few hours ago. *Signs of Approaching Death* warned that speech may be slurred or nonsensical; her speech was certainly hard to understand, but by no means nonsensical. The nurse and I strained to hear what she was trying to say. "She's asking for cream?" the nurse asked incredulously. "Ice cream?" "Cravings come and go," the pamphlet noted, but Margaret was not fond of ice cream, it seemed unlikely she would want some now. I bent over so my ear was close to her lips and asked her to repeat what she had said. She did, and it dawned on me after a moment that what she had said was, "Cremation."

"Yes," I said, "of course," and gave her a kiss.

I understood, people don't go in for open caskets in England much. A few years back Peter Banks, who had looked after our house for years, died. A big, robust middle-aged man, he came over after we had ridden every Saturday morning to have coffee with us in the tack room and find out what needed doing, accompanied by his black and white Australian sheep dog Faye. Faye was a large, exuberant, and friendly dog who sometimes used to ride in a crate attached to the pillion of Peter's Harley-Davidson; she was a working dog whose job was to chase the geese off the lawns of the Culinary Institute of America in Hyde Park, where Peter was in charge of maintenance. Margaret adored her, although when Faye saw someone she liked, she was apt to charge straight at you to be petted, and with her low center of gravity Faye could sometimes knock you down with her enthusiasm.

One Saturday morning Peter had his coffee, saw to a couple of things that Margaret wanted done, went home with Faye, and about an hour later we got a call from his ex-wife Joyce, a Hyde Park police officer, informing us that he had died in the kitchen of his house, which was not more than a quarter of an hour from ours. We were stunned—an hour ago he had been hale, hearty, cheerful, and then, suddenly, he was dead, a heart attack. When we went to the wake a few days later Peter was in his coffin, wearing his favorite Harley-Davidson T-shirt, with Faye sitting mournfully by the coffin greeting those she knew, this time without joyful exuberance—she knew death when she saw it. Peter's face was waxy; he looked like himself, certainly, but there was something gruesome about the makeup and the careful manicure. Peter was a man who worked with machinery, he always had a bit of grease under his fingernails, he didn't look "peaceful," as they like to say in the funeral business, he looked *dead*. We stood in line to pay our respects and when we reached the coffin and Margaret looked at him, she didn't cross herself or pray, she just paused, head bowed, then squeezed my hand hard and said, "Don't you *ever* do that to me."

The idea would never have crossed my mind. One of my favorite books when I was at school was Evelyn Waugh's *The Loved One*, with its hilarious send-up of American funeral practices, and I was at Simon & Schuster in 1963 when we published Jessica Mitford's best-selling *The American Way of Death*, a searing exposé of the American funeral industry. The last thing I would have done was put Margaret in an open casket, on display.

Margaret went back to sleep. "The patient becomes more tired, sleeping more and more," it noted in *Signs of Approaching Death*. "Fatigue" was apparently the seventh stage before death. I went outside for a breath of fresh air, where Bill Conklin, a friend and master plumber (he is actually a master of almost every trade, not just plumbing), was working. In a house as old as ours, even death cannot interrupt the occasional plumbing problem; in this case a septic issue. I had smelled it a couple of days ago, and asked Bill if he could take care of it without bringing in a back-hoe, so Margaret wasn't disturbed—nothing was more likely to upset her than the fact that we had a plumbing problem, except for a sick horse.

Bill had managed to find the problem, isolate it, and was just about to fix it. I said I was just about to make a pot of tea for myself, and asked if he would like some. He said yes, so I made two mugs of it and sat down next to him on a stone wall near the kitchen. We sipped in companionable silence. It was brisk outside, but not cold, spring at its best. Bill is a big man, and, like many big men, gentle and soft-spoken. I told him what Margaret was going through, and explained that from time to time I just needed a break. He understood, he knew about Margaret, then slowly he told me about the death of his son a few years back, who had been hit by a driver while riding his bicycle on the road outside the house. He had thought he would never recover from that, but he had, it had changed him, he never stopped thinking about it, but you had to go on, I would see. I was touched and moved, *comforted* in fact, by the story of a tragedy worse than mine, for what could be worse than the death of your child? One thing you can say for living in a small town: everyone has a tragedy and none of them is secret, or at least not secret for long.

The next day Marialice, one of the HVH nurses, came by to check on Margaret. She was tiny, trim, efficient, sympathetic, with the surprising strength that good nurses very often have; no matter how *petite* they may be, they can swiftly move or lift a patient, whatever his or her size and weight, and do it gently and smoothly. I enjoyed her visits, and Margaret responded to Marialice's presence, which always managed to soothe her. When Marialice was ready to go, I walked her out to her car, a white four-door sedan that seemed vaguely familiar. It wasn't until she was about open her door that I noticed the license plate—it was one I had seen around Pleasant Valley a hundred times, in the Acme supermarket parking lot or on my way to Dunkin' Donuts, a vanity plate with a message that Margaret and I had never been able to decipher. Some of them are easy, of course, as in "GOMETS" or "MUSTANG68," or Margaret's, which was "MEMSAHIB." For years I had "AUTHOR" until I got tired of people coming up to me at gas stations to tell me they had written a book. Others appear to be written in code, you see them briefly from behind and for hours afterward you try to figure out what they mean. I said that I had been trying to puzzle out the meaning of her license plate "MISUDAVE" for years, "I miss Dave," she said, which made sense once she had said it aloud. Dave was her son, she explained, he had been killed riding his bicycle on the road outside their house. "You're Bill Conklin's wife," I said, and for a moment we stood there in the driveway, with tears in our eyes, and gave each other a hug.

It was exactly one week before Margaret's death.

16.

ON GOOD FRIDAY, April 14, I summed up the situation for Christopher: "Margaret is dying, she is heavily sedated, bedridden . . . She has moments of consciousness, and speaks sometimes, but it's often hard to understand what she is trying to say. It may be a matter of days, maybe more, I hope not, but I think it is best for her to die at home, in her own bed . . . Don't call, her mind is still working, unfortunately, so it's hard for me to talk. I will call or email you with updates when I can. It is a nightmare . . . I am with her 24/7, cot set up outside the bedroom so I can come when she asks for me."

The dying can hear. *When Death Is Near* wisely warns the reader specifically of this. "Because hearing remains intact to the end . . . remember not to say anything in front of the person that you wouldn't say if he or she were awake." For this reason I was careful not to answer the telephone in the bedroom when people wanted a progress report, even when she appeared to be comatose. Margaret could hear what was said, there was no point to increasing her agitation by talking about her. I kept the progress reports short, and by email. I reported to a friend that Margaret was "trapped in the bedroom and the bed, unable to move, only the eyes show life . . . She is a prisoner of the disease, and is fighting it with all her strength, but that is a mixed blessing. She is now on medication given sublingually every 3/4 hours to calm her anxiety, plus morphine as needed. It is as bad as anything I can imagine, maybe worse since she can hear, and knows that she is dying. I wish I could end it for her."

Morphine "as needed" was the most important thing at this point. Giving it to Margaret every three hours meant eight pills a day. At that rate I would run out of morphine quickly, but HVH told me not to worry, I could have as much as Margaret needed. At this point, however, even giving Margaret her pills had become more difficult—her teeth were fiercely clenched, they had to be gently pried open, just far enough apart to slip the pill into her mouth on a tongue depressor and lodge it under her tongue to dissolve. Her 24/7 nurses, Sylvan, Tameca, Amber, Tashena, Sylvia, and Laura, were amazingly skilled at doing this without hurting her, although you could tell from Margaret's eyes that she didn't like having her teeth forced open—who would? Giving her any kind of nourishment or liquid was now even harder. The only way was to fill a syringe with Ensure or water, slip the needle between her teeth, and press the plunger very slowly so she didn't gag or choke.

Our old friend Tom Murray wanted to say goodbye to Margaret. I thought she wouldn't mind this—after all, he was a doctor, a professional as well as a friend like Colleen, she might not mind his seeing her in this state, and so it proved. Tom is a big man, and when he sat down next to Margaret she seemed to shrink to the size of a doll. He held her hand and talked to her quietly for almost half an hour, and the sound of his voice seemed to relax her. Perhaps not surprisingly he had a good bedside manner, he was one of the best ob-gyn physicians in Dutchess County, no doubt a soothing voice had been a significant asset in many a delivery or surgery. He and Margaret adored each other, although they often quarreled noisily and vehemently over dinner, mostly about horses. Tom owned racehorses, Margaret competed on hers. Although they were both Democrats, they argued about politics too, Tom was a friend of Nancy Pelosi's, Margaret had been close to Robert Kennedy and was on the presidential campaign trip in 1968 that ended in his assassination. However sharp the argument, they never left the restaurant without making up outside, although Margaret would often say as we were driving home, "I *still* say Tom doesn't know a thing about horses except how to bet on them." She never denied that Tom was good at that: he once won $199,000 on a $96 "pick six" bet, he routinely won "four pick bets," and he begins his day by reading the *Racing Forum.*

When he came out of the bedroom he had tears in his eyes. He wiped them away. "She's dehydrated," he said, resuming his professional manner with no apparent effort. "You might want to ask home hospice to put in an IV." I didn't want to call Donna over the Easter weekend, so I sent her an email telling her what Dr. Tom had said, and got back a stern but sensible reply within an hour. "Hydration is very difficult and not necessary at this point. Margaret is in the last stages and does not need to eat and drink. She should be kept comfortable with mouth swabs and good skin care, unfortunately many people may tell you otherwise at this time. If we do hydration it will only prolong her suffering."

"The last stages" brought me up short. I realized that not only I, but even Tom, a doctor, still imagined that Margaret was a "patient," and that she needed "treatment," like IV rehydration. It's a natural impulse: you see somebody who is dehydrated, your first instinct is to give liquids as soon as possible. But Margaret was not a sick patient, she wasn't going to get better, she was dying, the stark truth was that the more quickly she died, the better for her. I *knew* this, but on a subconscious level I hadn't *accepted* the consequences of it yet, I hadn't thought of what I was doing as *prolonging* her suffering, I thought of it as caring for her. Thom emailed me later that evening to reinforce Donna's message: "It is really in the patient's best interest to lovingly give her nothing. Anything that you can give her, food or drink cannot be absorbed or metabolized, and will most likely make her feel even worse . . . Donna and I and the other hospice nurses have seen hundreds and thousands of patients such as Margaret, believe us when we say, 'Just hold her hand.' "

This was not an easy message to absorb. Margaret wanted, or seemed to want, more Ensure, her eyes flickered toward the bedside table where a bottle of chocolate Ensure stood. Who can say no to someone they love who is dying? Later that night I asked Thom for his advice about the Ensure, and he replied, "Regardless of what Margaret demands you are the caregiver. You have to give her not necessarily what she wants but what is best for her. If she can swallow safely I would give her very small sips. The important thing is to keep her safe and comfortable, not an easy choice. If she coughs or chokes on the tiniest bit it would make her more uncomfortable."

I asked the nurse to inject a little chocolate Ensure between Margaret's teeth with a syringe, and luckily, after tasting it, she lost interest. It may have been just the taste of chocolate that she wanted, a reminder of the Cadbury's Fruit & Nut bars that she loved—whether or not it made her feel better, it made *me* feel better, but of course that was not the object.

A different source of concern was the beginning of a large bedsore on her left buttock, almost inevitable when the dying person is lying on her back almost twenty-four hours a day with all her systems, including circulation, in the process of shutting down. I had been warned that bedsores are awful, and it was true, they *are* awful, hard to look after, horrible to look *at*, raw, suppurating, oozing. As the body loses fat and muscle it loses its natural cushion against the pressure and friction of lying down. No matter how many pads and pillows you put under the patient's buttocks a bedsore is likely to appear, and once it does there is no getting rid of it, no matter how much DermaCerin and Aloe Vesta you slather on and massage in. Our friend Sandra Valenti went to Bed Bath & Beyond to buy wedge-shaped pillows that might make Margaret more comfortable, at the suggestion of one of the nurses, and the pillows seemed to help a bit, taking some of the pressure off her buttocks. Still, the bedsore was dismaying, a sign that Margaret's body was beginning to decay while she was still alive.

She was seldom conscious for long at this point, the morphine kept her sedated but restless. I spent most of the day sitting on the bed, holding her hand, feeling useless, but hoping Thom was right. Her hand felt alternately cold and hot—that too had been predicted in *When Death Is Near*, on page eight: "As the body becomes weaker, so does the temperature control mechanism in the brain." It was at once reassuring and alarming that Margaret's body was following the script, going through all the changes, or "transitions," as Donna called them, that HVH had predicted. Her mental state was hard to judge—when she woke from time to time she seemed frightened or angry, rather than suffering from "Confusion and Disorientation" as promised in the booklet—frightened at what was happening to her, angry perhaps that the rest of us were sitting around her more or less helplessly, and likely going to go on living after she was dead. *Why me?* is the unanswerable question of the dying, or perhaps more to the point, *Why me now?*

I remembered reading about the death of Atul Gawande's father in *Being Mortal*: "The suffering [he] experienced in his final day was not exactly physical, the medicine did a good job of preventing pain." It was what was in his father's *mind* that caused the pain, the knowledge that he was dying. None of us can know what this feels like until we get there, which most of us will, except for those who die instantly and without warning, or those who are so lost in senile dementia that they slip unaware into death. The vast majority of us will go as Margaret was going, knowing in some corner of the mind that we are moving inexorably into the unknown, floating away from life toward extinction, our mind awash in memories about to be forgotten forever, hopes for the future that will never be fulfilled, things we wish we'd never done, things that we'd hoped to do and never will, words that we wish we'd never spoken, words that we wish we could speak but it's now too late, fears for those we are about to leave behind, and for ourself.

Did she remember being given her first pony Snowy at the age of the four, Sunday dinners at Robin's Mill with her father and mother, the silverware gleaming on the table and her father cutting paper-thin slices of roast beef (Paul was a masterful sharpener of the carving knife and carver of paper-thin slices, and Margaret expected her husbands to be as well), her first love, the years in Kenya, her marriages? Did she remember how she used to be able to bring a room full of people to awed silence simply by sweeping in wearing white silk pants from Jax, skintight from the waist to the knees, belled below, and a black silk blouse without a bra (she never needed one)?

Perhaps her favorite song was Jim Morrison of the Doors singing "Twentieth Century Fox." "Well, she's fashionably lean / And she's fashionably late / She'll never wreck a scene / She'll never break a date / But she's no drag / Just watch the way she walks . . ." It might have been written with Margaret in mind, it was her theme song, at one time in her life she sang it as she walked around the apartment on Central Park West naked, "No tears, no fears / No ruined years, no clocks," she *was* "the queen of cool."

Did she remember the first time we made love after riding in Central Park in that same apartment, when I had to struggle to pull off her tight riding boots without a bootjack as she lay on the bed? In a marriage our own happy memories are not necessarily the same as those of the other person. That is perhaps the last secret we take with us.

~⁓

Dr. Gawande is right to remark that *his* father was "at peace in sleep, not in wakefulness"—so was Margaret. Awake, her hands began to tremble and she struggled to speak, often unable to find the word she was looking for or to pronounce it when she had. Asleep, her eyes closed, her breathing was calm—already slightly irregular, but not yet alarmingly so—she looked relaxed, perhaps dreaming of the past. It would have been nice if she had been carried toward death dreaming on an unbroken tide of happy memories, whatever they might have been, but it didn't happen, perhaps it doesn't happen to anyone unless they die in their sleep. I held her hand and talked to her about places we had been, things we had seen, dinner parties she had given in the days when she still gave formal candlelit dinner parties, black-tie, all her parents' silver on the table, the Spode red-and-gold-dragon-pattern china glinting in the candlelight, the Baccarat glasses that had to be hand-washed because they were too fragile to put in the dishwasher; about dinner parties we had gone to, about our trip to India, which had been a disaster, and our trips to Egypt, which we had both loved. I talked until I was hoarse, what mattered was the sound of my voice, not what I said. Silence increased her restlessness if she was awake; after all, she was about to get an eternity of it.

I waited for "the surge," the sudden, unexpected burst of energy that is supposed to precede death in what the HVH caregiver's guide calls "the end-of-life," a new experience for both of us. Margaret as far as I know had never attended a deathbed. I had seen plenty of people killed in the ten days I spent in Budapest during the 1956 Hungarian Revolution, but that's not at all the same thing as sitting for hours next to someone you love who is dying.

A day later the surge came at last, Margaret suddenly seemed to revive, her speech improved, thin and bedraggled as she was, she looked more like herself. If one hadn't known better, one might have thought she was recovering, but it was a cruel illusion. When I came back into the room after taking a short break, one of the nurses said that Margaret had been talking about hoses, did it mean that the tube of the catheter might be causing her pain? I sat down and listened to her carefully, and after a time I recognized the word "horses."

Of course Margaret would want to be reassured, above all things, that her horses would be looked after even though we had already made arrangements that this would happen, so I took her hand, which felt as thin-boned and fragile as a bird's wing, and promised her again that I would look after her horses, and the ghost of a smile passed across her face, following which the surge ended, her eyes closed, she slept.

I sent an email to Donna to say that Margaret was very quiet now, and weaker, although her breathing was still normal.

The next day, Donna came by in the morning for coffee. After she had examined Margaret I asked her how long Margaret had to live, a question I could not have imagined asking a year ago. It could be a matter of a few days, she thought, perhaps even only a few hours. Had I thought, she asked gently, about making the funeral arrangements?

As it happened, I had already been in touch with our local funeral home, so at lunchtime Dawn and I went down to meet

with the owner, Michael Sontheimer, and finalize the arrangements. As an admirer of Jessica Mitford's *The American Way of
Death*, I was expecting the kind of nerve-wracking, high-pressure
negotiation that accompanies the purchase of a new car, but nothing of the sort happened. Sontheimer was gracious, his manner
was sympathetic, he was businesslike and quick to put me at my
ease. I explained that Margaret wanted to be cremated, she did
not want to be embalmed or to have an open casket. He did not
try to talk me into or out of anything. She could be cremated, of
course, and her remains placed in any container I chose, and the
viewing, when it took place, could be focused on the container
rather than a casket. I leafed through the catalog of containers.
Are there really people who put their loved one's "cremains," as
they are called in the funeral trade, in a faux-magnum of Dom
Pérignon champagne, with the name and dates on the label? Nor
did I think Margaret would want to be placed in an elaborate urn
or a statue of an angel with unfurled wings and a screw-in base
either. I chose a simple polished wood box instead.

Apart from signing the contract there was nothing more to
do—Sontheimer would have the body picked up night or day as
soon as Margaret "passed," arrange for cremation as soon afterward as possible, collect the ashes, and arrange for the certificate
of death. Since I was a writer, I might want to have a stab at preparing an obituary, people often left this to the last moment, but
he thought it was best to be prepared. We exchanged a solemn
handshake and I returned home. It had not been difficult at all,
much easier than buying a car, although I felt some guilt, as if
I had betrayed Margaret by talking about her cremation while
she was still alive. Could I look her in the eye and say, *I was just
down in Pleasant Valley arranging for your funeral?*

But of course there was no need to do that, she was now fast asleep, the surge, such as it was, had passed. I went down and started to gather the information I needed for writing her obituary, and emailed our friend Carol Kozlowski, president of the United States Eventing Association, to get a list of Margaret's competition highlights over the years, conscious that it would be the thing she most wanted me to get right. Carol sent it at once, and I saw that from 1996 to 2006 Margaret had placed in the year-end awards nine times, five times winning national first place. "She was a force to be reckoned with, for sure," Carol commented when she emailed the list. More remarkably, Margaret was sixty-six years old when she won her last national first place, amazing in a tough, demanding, and dangerous sport where most winners are in their thirties and forties. It didn't take much time to write the obituary. I had been thinking of it for several days, and as a regular reader of the obituaries in the *New York Times*— as I get older I am always interested to see how many people in my age bracket have died, and whether I know any of them—I did not find it difficult to strike the right note. I wrote a long obituary for our local paper the *Poughkeepsie Journal* and a shorter one for the *Times*.

Upstairs, Margaret was much the same, asleep, which was surely a blessing, the only change was that her teeth were now so firmly clenched that giving her a pill was very difficult, nor did she react to having them pried open just wide enough for the nurse to slip the pill in and under her tongue. Over the next two days Margaret followed the "Signs and Symptoms of Approaching Death" to the letter, except for the one entitled "Saying Goodbye": there would be no opportunity to "share forgiveness, or let go of past conflicts," as the booklet put it, nor to "share expressions of gratitude." Otherwise, all followed in exact order as the booklet predicted: restlessness, difficulty swallowing, further discoloration of the skin, ongoing changes in breathing, rattling breath sounds, weak pulse, further decrease in blood pressure, decreased urine output, eyelids no longer able to close completely. Well, no rattling sounds as yet, but the changes in breathing were the most difficult to bear, it was as if she were struggling silently for breath. She no longer tried to speak, but her eyes were partly open, staring at some point above the fireplace that faced her. She could still see and hear; it was fearful to imagine what must be going on in her mind despite the Valium, Haldol, Ativan, and morphine. Did any of it reduce or obliterate her knowledge of what was happening to her? Perhaps, her eyes did not reflect terror or fear; I would like to think that they showed resignation, the recognition that the struggle was coming to an end, perhaps even gratitude that it was so. But it may be that we simply read what we want to in the eyes of someone we love who is dying, we want them to go peacefully, and therefore we see in their eyes the sign that they *are* at peace. They can no longer contradict us, they can no longer blame us for having been unable to help or for anything else. If they are focused on anything, they become, at a certain point, focused inward.

Was Margaret saying to herself, *I am Margaret, I am, I am, you can't take that away from me*—but of course death can and does, and was about to do so. Death, I reflected, is the most democratic of human experiences, we are all going there eventually, even the richest, the most beautiful, and the luckiest among us, nobody can buy their way out of it.

Priscilla, the kindly, patient HVH aide who gave Margaret her sponge bath every two days, came that afternoon to bathe Margaret, but Margaret was unresponsive, in fact hardly seemed to notice that it was happening. I stayed, holding her hand, helping to give Margaret her medications, until late that night when I finally lay down on my cot outside the room. I was too tired, or too emotionally exhausted, *not* to sleep, although I was still wearing my clothes, but I was woken early in the morning by a series of long, urgent, terrible cries. I rushed into the bedroom, and looked at the nurse. She shook her head; whoever was crying, it wasn't Margaret. Ruby was curled up on the bed beside Margaret, fast asleep.

I looked at my watch, it was five in the morning. I could still hear the cries, louder now, and more urgent. I went downstairs, following the noise, turning on the lights as I made my way toward the kitchen. There, in the laundry room, Kit Kat was lying squeezed in the V-shaped space between the door and the wall, in obvious pain. I tried to put her on her feet, but she gave a piercing scream and was unable to move her back legs at all. I did not want to leave Margaret, but I knew what she would have wanted me to do or would have done herself. So I went upstairs, explained what had happened to the nurse, grabbed a blanket from the linen closet, wrapped Kit Kat in the blanket as gently as I could, and took her out to the car. Kit Kat had always had great presence, yet when I picked her up it felt as if she had shrunk to nothing.

It had been many years since Margaret and I had last been in the emergency veterinary clinic off Route 55 in Poughkeepsie, and I wasn't sure I could find it in the dark by myself without Margaret to do the navigating, nor was I even certain it was still in the same place and open 24/7, but it was. A kind vet examined Kit Kat. She thought the cat might have had a heart attack and fallen from the kitchen counter or wherever she had been and broken her pelvis. Kit Kat had been a hugely ambitious jumper, she took such big leaps (and broke so many objects that were in her way on tables and countertops) that we called her "the Flying Cat." The vet said she could try to repair the pelvis, but . . . Her expression made it clear that it would be hopeless. Kit Kat was over fourteen, there seemed no reason to put her through the trauma of surgery. I sighed and asked her to put the cat down. I hoped Margaret would have done the same.

I left at daybreak and drove home in the bleak dawn through

empty streets lit by orange streetlights. I could see no reason to tell Margaret; even if she understood, it could only add to her woes, so what was the point? Her breath was now irregular and noisy, followed by long pauses during which she hardly seemed to be breathing at all. I sat holding her hand through the day. When Sylvan arrived at eight o'clock that night to begin his shift, he took one look at her and sighed. He was a professional, he knew what he was looking at.

I did too that night. When the "death rattles" finally came, they were not as loud or as dramatic as they are sometimes described in fiction (and even in nonfiction), but they were distinct, and unmistakable for anything else.

I gave her a kiss. I have no idea whether or not she knew it, there was no sign that she felt it, it was as if her whole being were being consumed in the death rattles. I dozed for a few minutes, then I felt Sylvan shake my shoulder gently. I guessed what was coming. Margaret's breaths had become shallower, with longer pauses between each one, and finally at one-fifteen in the morning on Saturday, April 22, the pause grew longer and went on without interruption, no breath came.

Sylvan leaned over, closed her eyelids, and said, "She's gone."

AFTERWORD

I worried a lot. Will the garden grow, will the rivers
flow in the right direction, will the earth turn
as it was taught, and if not how shall
I correct it?

Was I right, was I wrong, will I be forgiven,
can I do better?

Will I ever be able to sing, even the sparrows
can do it and I am, well,
hopeless.

Is my eyesight fading or am I just imagining it,
am I going to get rheumatism,
lockjaw, dementia?

Finally I saw that worrying had come to nothing.
And gave it up. And took my old body
and went out into the morning,
and sang.

—MARY OLIVER,
"I Worried"

LATE THAT NIGHT, after two men from the funeral home had taken her body away just as smoothly and unobtrusively as promised, I sent a message to everyone who needed to know that Margaret had "died peacefully at 1:15 a.m."

It is what one writes, it's the standard phrase, like ending a letter with, "Sincerely."

Dying, or "passing," as so many people prefer to call it, is a process, death the completion of the process. The truth is that I don't know whether Margaret died peacefully or not. She died quietly . . . after the death rattles her breathing slowed and grew fainter until it stopped.

Over the last few weeks of her life, her body, as Donna Engle predicted, started to shut down, whole systems simply failed, the body closed down organ after organ trying to preserve the spark of life at the core for as long as possible. Breathing, and with it the heart, are the last to stop, and then we are gone, to wherever or nowhere. Whether the experience was peaceful or not, who can say? Certainly, we all want a peaceful death, a painless transition into the unknown, and perhaps Margaret had one. I hope so.

It took Margaret almost exactly a year to die, if measured from her diagnosis until her death, but of course the process had begun years before, with the first appearance of the melanoma and her hesitation to have it biopsied, the enemy was already within the gates. Perhaps even five years ago it had already been too late to stop it from digging in somewhere in the body until it was ready to metastasize.

One is left only with questions. Should she have had the patch on her cheek biopsied instead of covering it with makeup? Most certainly so. Should she have been told that she needed to have a PET scan once a year after the melanoma surgery? Very likely, but perhaps we should have thought of it ourselves. Was it worth having the second brain surgery after the tumors returned? Hard to say; she would have died sooner, and perhaps more unpleasantly, without the surgery. Certainly Margaret was mistaken to choose radiation instead of a second brain surgery when the tumor returned—she ended up having to undergo the second brain surgery anyway, and by then it was too late, she only lived for two months after it.

We should have moved faster, we should have done this, we should have done that, perhaps Margaret should have been pushed harder into trying immunotherapy once everything else had failed, but you can't push someone further than he or she is willing to go, and by that time it was clear to Margaret that whatever happened, the life she knew wasn't going to come back, she wasn't going to ride with the wind in her hair again, and she had the courage to recognize when she had had enough. One can torment oneself endlessly about what we might have done, but ultimately the person who has the cancer has to decide if and when to surrender, and do it knowingly, without guilt or blame.

At some point after the second brain surgery and the Gamma Knife radiation, it was clear to Margaret that she wasn't going to get better, that the equivalent of a miracle at Lourdes wasn't an option, and she decided she was going to die at home in her own bed, with her cats beside her, and who can say that she was wrong?

Not me.

ACKNOWLEDGMENTS

My thanks to Lynn Nesbit and to Robert Weil, without whose enthusiasm and support this book would never have been written, to my dear friend and assistant Dawn Lafferty, who lived through the experience with me, and to Colleen Sinon for her unstinted help and friendship. This book will serve as a tribute and a gesture of thanks to all Margaret's caregivers, but especially to Donna Engle, Laura Sanders and Thom Schwartz, to Brooke Newman for reading every chapter and for her constant encouragement, and above all to Alain C. J. de Lotbinière, M.D., doctor and gentleman.

ABOUT THE AUTHOR

MICHAEL KORDA lives on a farm in Dutchess County, New York, in a small town whose most distinguishing features are a supermarket and a Dunkin' Donuts, and which he wrote about in *Country Matters*. Editor-in-chief emeritus of Simon & Schuster, he is also the author of *Queenie, Horse People*, and *Charmed Lives*.